West Academic Publishing's
Law School Advisory Board

The First Amendment

Robert C. Power
Associate Dean for Academic Affairs,
Distinguished Professor of Law
Widener University Commonwealth Law School

Mark C. Alexander
Professor of Law and Associate Dean for Academics
Seton Hall University School of Law

A SHORT & HAPPY GUIDE® SERIES

WEST
ACADEMIC
PUBLISHING

a short & happy guide series is a trademark registered in the U.S. Patent and Trademark Office.

© 2016 LEG, Inc. d/b/a West Academic

      444 Cedar Street, Suite 700
      St. Paul, MN 55101
      1-877-888-1330

Printed in the United States of America

ISBN: 978-1-63460-258-7

Acknowledgments

Bob thanks Charles and Jane Power, sorry that this is later rather than sooner. He thanks Paula Heider and Jeremy Wingert for their excellent help telling him what to do. He also wishes to acknowledge the work of various research assistants over the years, and specifically thanks Harrison Carruthers and Amanda Tarpitt as class representatives.

Mark thanks Tracy Alexander for encouraging and inspiring him to do this book. Many thanks to his beloved family; too many to single out any one, but deeply grateful for all. He is also grateful for support and assistance from Seton Hall University School of Law, its students, faculty and staff.

Both of us thank the excellent production staff at West Academic. You were superb to work with.

Table of Contents

A Short & Happy Guide to the First Amendment

CHAPTER 1

Introduction

The First Amendment is in many ways a defining feature of our government. Coming after the Constitution itself creates the structure of government, the Amendments in large part spell out individual rights. The First Amendment protects the freedom of religion, speech and press, and the right to assemble and petition the Government. It transforms the Great Document from simply being about the government, to being about the people and their freedoms.

The problems we encounter in talking about the First Amendment are always interesting. They typically present situations with which we can easily identify, whether an individual's attempt to protest government policy, to one's desire to worship without interference, to what we see on television and online. The specific cases are—like *Law & Order*—ripped from the headlines, as we talk about flag-burning, curse words, pornography, Ten Commandments displays, prayer in schools, campaign finance, and more. The specific problems are always interesting and challenging, like a good puzzle.

Interestingly, it all starts with the words "Congress shall make no law", thus apparently applying an absolute ban on the federal government regulating these areas. Instead, we will see that the First Amendment has been interpreted broadly to apply to all governments, federal, state and local. And what may at first appear to be an absolute ban has been interpreted to allow very significant restrictions on speech, religion and the press.

A. The Meaning of the First Amendment— Speech

We want to start with a broad philosophical discussion of what the First Amendment is about, to set up all that follows throughout these pages. In this book, we focus most heavily on speech and religion. Starting with speech, there are several broad, important themes that will be important for you to understand as we move forward. The basic question is *Why do we provide for a protection of speech in this country?* There are several possible answers, none of which is exclusive, and each of which is complementary to the others.

1. Truth and the Marketplace of Ideas

First, we might consider the First Amendment to be essential to the pursuit of truth in a marketplace of ideas. The government is not allowed to interfere with this market, so as to let good ideas rise and fall on their merits. So, for example, if I want to argue that the earth is flat, then I can. I believe it to be true. I am convinced. I approach you and tell you that if you look out from where you are standing, across the horizon, you can see that the earth comes to an end, and it's a flat line out there. Think about it. It looks kinda flat to the naked eye. It ends, and when you get to the end, that's it. Flat. So you say that you are starting to believe me. Your search for the truth about our land is that it is flat. But then another friend comes up to you and says that you shouldn't listen to me. The earth is ROUND, she says! Amazing concept. How does she know? She has been on an airplane and could tell that there's something not quite flat from way up high. So you ask her, if she's sure, does she have any pictures. She says no, but she's pretty sure. You're not convinced yet. The debate is going on in your head. Finally an old man comes up to you and tells you he is from Montclair, New Jersey. Buzz Aldrin is his name. He has been up to the moon in a space ship, and guess what he saw? The earth, round, like a big blue marble in space. And he's got pictures to prove it. So now, you change your mind, and you believe the earth is round. By allowing all of us to speak, uninhibited, the marketplace of ideas sorted out this little debate, and you found what you believe to be true—that the earth is in fact round. The First Amendment ensures that we can always have such debates.

2.   *Self-Government and Robust Public Debate*

Another way to look at the importance of the First Amendment is to view it as central to our nation's commitment to self-governance through robust public debate. We as a people are committed to a system of government by which we are all allowed (and maybe even expected) to participate in governance. We threw away the mantle of monarchy in exchange for a government of the people, a democracy. In that context, it is essential for us all to participate, and for our participation **not** to be regulated by the government. Every day we are allowed to debate the policies of the government—good, bad or indifferent. President Obama wakes up each morning and looks out the window and can see *someone* out front on 1600 Pennsylvania Avenue with a sign that says *Impeach Obama* or *Obama Sucks*, or something like that. Before him, George W. Bush got to see protestors with the same message of ousting *him* from office, as did Bill Clinton before him, and so on and so on. The First Amendment protects that right, and prohibits the president or any government official from getting in the way of our self-governance.

That is in many ways a risk that all elected officials run. They have earned the power from some majority, but they must also respect those who disagree, in the minority. When we want to debate the key issues of the day, (as with the marketplace of ideas rationale), we let the political process work. We debate taxes, war, educational policy, and more. Every citizen is allowed to participate—it is all part of our self-governance, and the First Amendment ensures that the debate is robust and uninhibited.

3. *Individual   Autonomy   and   Liberty;   Self-Fulfillment*

A third way to look at the importance of the First Amendment is that it helps develop individual autonomy, fosters self-fulfillment, and enhances individual liberty. Seen this way, the First Amendment is all about helping the individual become the best possible person. It is the flip side of the first two ideas, but with a focus on the individual's growth, as opposed to a greater dialogue for all people, or broad self-governance. It is completely connected with those perspectives, as the marketplace of ideas does not function without strong-minded individuals, nor can we self-govern without a debate among engaged active participants. But still, we may look at the First Amendment as playing an essential role in the development of the *individual* to take an active role in this debate of ideas. With the individual free to participate without interference from the government, the individual grows through her membership in the collective dialog.

4. *Shield*

One final way for us to consider the First Amendment for our discussion is as a shield against the government. In this sense, we place the First Amendment in the context of the Bill of Rights, as an overarching protector of a sphere of privacy for the individual. In this context, whether religion or speech, the First Amendment protects the individual's most private and personal thoughts and beliefs, and the expression thereof. By prohibiting the government from regulating individual speech, the First Amendment provides a protective shield around the individual to think and express herself without fear of censorship or retribution. This sphere of protection is essential to the individual's growth and participation in our society.

As you can probably see even more clearly now, all these conceptions go together, one feeding the other. You need not pick or choose one, but you must consider all and which perspective you find most compelling, in order to most thoroughly understand and analyze First Amendment doctrine. By the end, you will likely have a preferred theory, or an order in which these ideas fit. For now, think about them, and apply these concepts as you read the cases we discuss going forward.

B. Analytical Framework

Having talked about the broad philosophical issues, we want to set forth a bit more practical analytical approach to the problems you will see in this book and throughout First Amendment analysis.

1. Preliminary Questions: Expression, State Action

First, we have preliminary questions about speech itself. While the First Amendment protects the freedom of "speech," we often are not dealing with the spoken word. So we will see that we must instead look at "expression" or "expressive activities". Sometimes we look at a speech, sometimes a written word. Sometimes we see people burning flags and draft cards and crosses. Marches, rallies and protests, with signs, armbands, and yes, speeches, are also covered. The key is to look for that expressive element.

Next, we want to make sure that the state is involved in some way—this is a *state action* problem—basic doctrine you should have learned in Con Law. The freedom of expression is a freedom from *government* action or suppression, but the Constitution just doesn't care about private action. For example, when they were younger sometimes Mark's children would make a big fuss in the car—lots of talking, annoying, etc. When he would tell them to be quiet, when they felt clever they would respond, *It's the First Amendment, I can say what I want.* Mark would reply, *In my car, and in my house, I set the rules, and there's no freedom of speech. Outside this car, you can say what you want and the government can't shut you down.* (It never was very successful, but it did indoctrinate the children!!) Point is: without state action, the protections of the First Amendment won't apply.

2. *Absolute*

Next, we briefly ask why the First Amendment is not an absolute bar on government regulation of speech. After all, the text says "Congress shall make *no* law," so why can Congress make *any* law restricting the freedom of speech? Justice Hugo Black was famous for urging that position, but he never prevailed and the Court has made clear that the First Amendment does not provide an absolute ban on government regulation of speech, religion, etc. Still, you should ask yourself why the Framers put this strong mandate in the forefront of the Bill of Rights, if not for it to have some very serious restrictions on the power of government to regulate our beliefs, thoughts, and expression.

3. Balancing

In the absence of an absolute approach to the First Amendment, as in much of Constitutional Law, much analysis turns on balancing. In these cases we balance the interest of the state in regulating expressive conduct against the individual right to free expression. For example, while an individual may have a right to sing, as expressive conduct, we also understand that the people have a right to some quiet, so that the government may regulate the time, place and manner of any concerts. There is often a balance of that sort struck when we analyze how the government may regulate particular expressive activity. We will discuss some of these issues throughout, but most notably in Chapter 3.

4. Content-Based and Content-Neutral Regulation

We will also discuss another important concept throughout: content-neutrality. We will consider times where speech regulations are content-based, and times where such regulation is content-neutral. To start that discussion, we first consider the concept of *viewpoint neutrality.* You can probably understand very easily that the government cannot regulate speech based on the speaker's viewpoint or point-of-view. It's almost so obvious that it goes without saying: the government cannot pick and choose to silence people who express a particular point of view. Otherwise, the government could allow all those who support its policies to speak, and those who don't could be silenced. That is too reminiscent of the notorious example of the King locking up all his critics. We threw off that practice, and the First Amendment protects the individual who dares to speak truth to power.

We also must realize that the government can entrench its own power not just by silencing speakers based on their perspective, but also based on the subject matter. If the president's policies on a particular matter are unpopular, he could say that there will be no debate on that subject. In that situation, the president would not be silencing any one speaker, and would not be silencing any one point-of-view. But by taking the entire subject off the table, he would in effect be silencing more of his critics than supporters. Again, the president would be protecting his own power by suppressing the speech of his opponents. So the First Amendment does not allow either *viewpoint-based* or *content-based* regulation of speech.

5. *Categorization*

Having established that the First Amendment is not absolute, so the government *can* regulate speech, there are still some expressive activities that enjoy lesser, or even no First Amendment protection. That's the concept of categorization. Case law has developed such that certain categories of expressive activity are not considered to be protected expression under the First Amendment. The important result that follows is that expressive activities in these categories are *not* protected from government regulation as would other forms of speech. We will explore each of these categories in Chapter 2. For now, note that these are the six main categories of unprotected or less-protected speech:

    a.   Incitement

    b.   Fighting Words

    c.   Libel

    d.   Hate Speech

    e.   Sexually-Explicit Expression

    f.   Commercial Speech

6. *Forum Analysis*

Our last introductory piece on free speech is forum analysis. The constitutionality of government regulation of speech can depend on the forum in which the speech takes place. The quintessential example of protected public speech is the street-corner speaker. Imagine a person standing on a street corner or in a park trying to spread the word on the important issues of the day. In public, on that street corner or park, the speaker is generally allowed to speak—it is a traditional public forum. The government may regulate the time, place and manner, but it may not restrict the speech altogether (and it certainly may not do so based on content). A second category is a designated public forum, where the government opens public space to speech activity even though it is not a traditional public forum. Public theaters, schools, and universities often fall into this category. If the government opens it to speech, then it must be open to all on an equal basis, without regard to subject or viewpoint. But the government may also close the designated forum at any time. Similarly, the government may limit the forum to speakers based on some content, for example, making school rooms available only to speakers who will speak on school-related business; still, viewpoint restrictions are impermissible. Finally, in nonpublic fora, like airports, the government may restrict speech with very little restrictions, as long as they don't exercise viewpoint-based controls. These different fora also raise questions of levels of scrutiny, and we will consider those issues as we go forward. And finally, if the speech is not on any sort of government property, First Amendment restrictions do not protect the speaker—the Constitution just doesn't care.

C. The Meaning of the First Amendment— Religion

In one sense, the religion clauses are simpler to discuss because there is only one subject involved—religion. Speech, press, association, assembly, petitioning the government can be about anything or everything, and the First Amendment has to be interpreted to apply in each situation. The religion clauses focus on one thing, protecting religious beliefs, and they do it very well.

That is not to say that the religion clauses are clear or easy to apply. The question, *what is religion,* fills entire college philosophy courses and appears in a series of fascinating Supreme Court decisions. Chapter 8 addresses this question in a way that suggests its complexity while giving direction to resolving it in the majority of cases. That chapter then addresses the Free Exercise clause, the textual basis for our freedom of religious thought, belief, and practices. The Free Exercise clause presents in a very few words our national commitment to treat religion as a private, individual decision. As a matter of constitutional law, the Free Exercise clause serves to protect persons who hold religious beliefs *and* those who reject religious beliefs. Majority, minority, and idiosyncratic religious beliefs—and lack of any religious belief at all—are all protected from government restrictions in most situations. One complicating aspect of contemporary Free Exercise problems is the role of federal and state statutes. Although the Free Exercise clause protects many religious practices, Congress and many states have expanded those protections by statute. Such laws are almost always praised in the abstract, but can lead to difficult problems in application, such as the force of anti-discrimination laws against exclusionary practices that are rooted in religious beliefs, such as opposition to same-sex marriage.

The Establishment Clause is a counterweight to the Free Exercise clause. While the original intention may have been only to prevent the federal government from designating a state religion, it has long served as the theoretical basis for preventing governments from meddling in religious affairs. The majority of Establishment Clause controversies involve government efforts to help religion, either by financially supporting religious activities or by giving it a special role in government services or events. It is no surprise, therefore, to see religious leaders decry court decisions enforcing the Establishment Clause. By and large, Establishment Clause case law attempts to police a line between *permitted* actions (such as accommodating religion and making sure that religious activities are not disadvantaged), and *prohibited* actions (such as giving religious groups extra advantages). One of the trickiest aspects of the judicial role involves the status of "non-religion." Does government improperly disadvantage religion when it supports a non-religious theory, such as evolution, or does it improperly advantage religion when it supports education of faith-based theories, such as creationism?

At the heart of judicial interpretation of the religion clauses is the tightrope that governments must walk in order to comply with both requirements. Government must take care to allow often-obscure religious practices that the majority of people sometimes find strange and offensive. There is room to disallow religious practices, of course, where such practices cause real harm to society. But with minor exceptions, the overriding principle is to tolerate religious practices. From the other end, however, government is pressed not to elevate religious practices in a way that communicates government approval of specific religious practices or even religion in general. The lines drawn between these principles, and the factual distinctions identified in the case law, are often unclear and uncertain. This is exacerbated by the fact that some observers see government as hostile to their beliefs. For example, those who oppose any government subsidies of religious activities may interpret any such government support as showing hostility to non-religious persons, and those who support such subsidies may see any opposition to subsidies as hostility to religion.

D. Analytical Framework

To some extent, religion clause problems can be analyzed under a rubric similar to that for speech.

1. The first step is to identify the government action being challenged. As with speech (and almost all other constitutional rights), the law protects persons from government action, not private action. Thus, a private person, perhaps a boss, can discriminate against an employee on religious grounds, *at least as a matter of constitutional law.* (Statutes can and often do protect people from private discrimination.)

2. The next step is to examine how the government action causes a problem for the individual. Does the government action prohibit something she does for religious reasons? If so there is at least a free exercise argument. Does the government action make it more difficult to do something she does for religious reasons? This too is likely to be a free exercise issue, although there can be a major difference between prohibiting a practice and just making it more difficult. Does the government grant religion (either in general or a specific religion) a special status? That may be establishing religion.

3. If the problem is Free Exercise, there is a checklist to examine. Does the law explicitly single out and disadvantage a religious practice? If so, the law must withstand *strict scrutiny.* You already know a fair amount about strict scrutiny from Con Law. (By the end of this book the two of you will be good friends.) Is the law directed at religious practices? That is, regardless of its form, was the intention of the law's drafters to burden religious practices? If so, the law must withstand strict scrutiny. On the other hand, does

the law apply generally, to all persons, and was it adopted for a purpose unrelated to religion? Such laws are not subject to heightened scrutiny, at least as a matter of constitutional law, but are permitted by the Free Exercise clause if they satisfy Minimal or Rational Basis Scrutiny. There is still one more step in the Free Exercise area. Does a statute impose a greater restriction on government action that burdens religious practices? Numerous federal and state laws require that government actions that burden religious practices satisfy Strict Scrutiny even where the constitutional requirement would be rational basis.

4. If the problem is Establishment, there is a totally different checklist. First, determine whether the action falls into any of several categories that have specific tests or typical outcomes. For example, an official state prayer is probably unconstitutional without much further analysis. Similarly, financial support to education generally in which religious schools participate is probably constitutional. If you can't find a category directly on point, there are backup approaches. The one that carries the most official doctrinal "cred" is a three-part test the Supreme Court adopted in 1971. It provides that in order to be valid, a law must 1) have a secular (non-religious) purpose; 2) the primary effect must neither advance nor hinder religion; and 3) the law must not create excessive entanglement of government and religion. If that test doesn't lead you to a clear answer, (and don't be surprised if it doesn't), there are other principles individual opinions have relied on in evaluating actions challenged under the Establishment Clause. For example, does the law send a message that government approves a particular religion or practice? If so, some cases would characterize the problem of one of government "endorsement" or even "coercion" of religion. Others look simply to neutrality, some form of an even playing field. Application of the tests and principles is as likely to result in an argument as.in an answer. As you know by now, that is what the Constitution does best.

E. Structure of the Book

With this brief theoretical and conceptual introduction, in the remainder of the book, we will cover the First Amendment along the following lines. We spend chapters 2-6 discussing key aspects of free speech, then in chapter 7, we look mainly at press issues. What you will see is that the speech chapters practically form a flow chart for solving problems, so that there is a practical way to analyze free speech problems. In addition, throughout it all you will also be able to apply these theoretical frameworks to each problem, to understand more about why these opinions reach the results they do.

Chapters 8 and 9 look at freedom of religion, specifically the Free Exercise and Establishment clauses. Chapter 10 concludes our journey into the First Amendment.

As we go along, we are always reminded that this class is a part of Constitutional Law. Sometimes it is taught as part of a required Con Law course, and sometimes it is billed as a separated advanced Con Law class. As such, above all, we discuss the First Amendment to the Constitution itself, as expounded by the Justices in Supreme Court decisions. Studying the First Amendment involves constant reading and re-reading these opinions written over the past 200+ years. These decisions are written by people who have devoted themselves to the exercise of constitutional interpretation, but who don't always agree on the way to carry out that exercise or on the conclusions that exercise elicits. So as we read casebooks, we see majority opinions. But we also see concurring and dissenting opinions. Sometimes there's not even a majority, so we see a plurality. Only rarely do we read unanimous opinions—there is always a range of ways to answer the questions put before the court. That is all very interesting, but it means that we have few short rules and more long discussions.

So in order to keep this short and happy, we have a basic framework for how we present the material. We start with a basic discussion of key principles and cases. But this is not a treatise, hornbook or casebook. We expect that you will be reading your casebook, and you will be taking the time to brief cases, etc. After the discussion of the case, principle, etc., we will typically ask (and answer), **What is the Takeaway?** That will be our way of presenting something essential about the case—maybe a three-part test, maybe one clear rule, but maybe something more abstract. And then we will ask (and answer), **Why do we read and discuss this?** The cases themselves provide lots of ideas and opinions, and there is rarely one right answer. So the key thing for you is to know what the various perspectives are, as presented in the different opinions, and that reflects the philosophical framework we have set forth earlier. As we ask the *why* question, we hope that in addition to reading our answers, you will challenge our perspectives and also start to think about your own. At the end of each chapter we will highlight a few key points, framed as *Things to Know* and *Things to Think About*.

CHAPTER 2

Categorical Exceptions to First Amendment Protections

You believe in free speech as much as anyone else, but some things are just *too much*. You log on to your computer and a link attracts your attention: "Neo-Nazis Get Tough." It takes you to a speech by the head of the American Nazi Party arguing in favor of a race war. You then check your social media. One of your classmates has posted that his lab partner cheats on both his homework and his girlfriend. You know that can't be true. Does the Constitution protect such speech?

Maybe it doesn't. There are several categories that the Supreme Court has **excluded** from the First Amendment (courts tend to use "exceptions" and "exclusions" interchangeably). Although some of the cases are hard, they raise important questions, and can be boiled down to a few key tests and rules, subject to the universal rule in Constitutional Law that some matters are always in doubt— the "*it depends*" rule. There are three universally recognized categories: **incitement**, **defamation**, and **obscenity**. Several different descriptions of highly offensive communications vie for acceptance as a fourth categorical exception. A wholly different category—commercial speech—receives some protection, although it was once thought to be outside of First Amendment protection.

A. Incitement

Maybe the Nazi's speech was incitement, and excluded from First Amendment protection.

Most casebooks start with incitement, and much of modern First Amendment law developed from early cases addressing this category. These cases originated the most significant First Amendment speech doctrine, the clear and present danger test, and the dominant speech metaphor, "shouting fire in a theater."

Over about eight months in 1919, the Supreme Court decided several cases involving prosecutions under the Espionage Act—the same law at issue today concerning unauthorized disclosure of classified documents. Each case presented some form of opposition to the military during World War I, and the Court rejected all First Amendment claims. In *Schenk v. United States* (1919) (Holmes), the Court considered a First Amendment defense by leaders of the Socialist Party. They were charged with obstructing recruitment for the war because they mailed leaflets encouraging men to resist the military draft. For the majority, Justice Oliver Wendell Holmes wrote **"the most stringent protection of free speech would not protect a man in falsely shouting fire in a theater and causing a panic."** This statement alone makes *Schenk* an important milestone. The phrase makes the point that speech that causes serious harm may be limited. **The shout must not be true**, although the phrase is sometimes misquoted as "shouting fire in a crowded theater." *Truthfully* shouting fire would be praiseworthy. **The shout must also cause a panic.** Without a panic, there would be no stampede for the exits, and therefore no harm. Falsely shouting fire in an empty theater is not dangerous, and therefore would be protected.

These concepts are then encapsulated in Holmes's conclusion that **words may be punished when they constitute a "Clear and Present Danger"** of causing a harm that government is authorized to prevent. Remember this phrase.

In another of the World War I cases, *Abrams v. United States* (1919), Holmes refined the test, this time in dissent. Espionage Act charges were brought against a person who distributed leaflets advocating a general strike that would have shut down a munitions factory (the workers ignored the leaflets and continued their work). Abrams's purpose was to obstruct military action against the Red Army in Russia. **What's the Takeaway?** Justice Holmes was joined by Justice Brandeis to argue that the First Amendment allows government to intervene only in the face of **"clear and imminent danger."** More important than this minor change of terminology, however, was the explanation for recognizing strong speech protection for dissenting policy views. Abrams was incapable of harming the war effort: his speech was "a silly leaflet by an unknown man." Even direct incitement to crime is protected if it is harmless. Then Holmes added another ingredient to free speech analysis—and this is **why we read this case.** Government should not stop people from arguing to change government policies. **The country is best served by allowing all views to be expressed, even those we detest, so that the best ideas—the truth—will prevail. This policy of the "marketplace of ideas" recurs in many of the Supreme Court's First Amendment cases.**

After fifty years of fine-tuning the various opinions of the World War I cases, the Supreme Court restated the test in a case that dominates today. In *Brandenburg v. Ohio* (1969), the state convicted a Ku Klux Klan leader for advocating violence against African Americans, Jews, and government officials that "suppress" whites. The Court followed the clear and present danger principle, recognizing that it had been reshaped over the years. **The new** version of the test was that government may punish advocacy of force or violation of the law only if the speech is "directed to inciting or producing imminent unlawful action and is likely to incite or achieve such action." Abstract support of violence (or other lawbreaking) is protected speech unless there is actual incitement to action in the very near future. In this case, the threat of violence was put off to some uncertain time and was too general to be clear. It was neither **imminent** nor **likely to produce** violence.

What's the Takeaway? In *Brandenburg,* the Court relied on all three bases of Holmes's analysis. The First Amendment does not protect words that are directly connected to harmful action, such as those that maliciously cause a human stampede. But it does protect those words unless:

- the speaker has the intent to (the speech is directed to)

- cause dangerous or criminal behavior (inciting or producing unlawful action)

- the harm is present (at least imminent)

- the harm is clear (likely).

The elements are jumbled and the words are modified, but they remain essentially intact. **Why do we read and discuss this?** The emphasis on the protection of abstract advocacy illustrates the marketplace of ideas principle—allow all speakers, including very unhappy citizens, to speak out, and the now-informed public will accept those ideas that are worthy. Think of it as constitutional crowd-sourcing.

Brandenburg was essentially a unanimous decision, and no cases since then have caused the Court to retreat. *Brandenburg* states the general principle for incitement. Advocacy of violence or lawbreaking is unpleasant or worse, but unless the language is likely to cause harm very soon, the First Amendment protects it. More importantly for First Amendment analysis generally, the "shouting fire" metaphor, the restated clear and present danger test, and the marketplace principle were solidified as part of a more general collection of First Amendment principles, and now pop up in areas removed from incitement.

B. Defamation

Let's go back to our example from the beginning of the chapter about your classmate's online post about his lab partner. What's the legal liability there? Your classmate may be liable for **defamation**.

The second categorical exception to the First Amendment is defamation. The common law of torts allows recovery of presumed and punitive damages for defamation where a speaker (slander) or writer (libel) makes a false statement that injures the plaintiff's reputation. Defamation was traditionally excluded from First Amendment protection because defamatory speech is false, and false statements were thought to have no value. The intricacies of tort doctrine made this very broad exclusion problematic in several respects, most notably a legal presumption that defamatory statements *were* false, which meant that even *truthful* speakers had to convince a jury that the statement was true to avoid liability.

In *New York Times v. Sullivan* (1964) (Brennan), the Supreme Court expanded speech protection by narrowing the exclusion for defamation. A police commissioner in Montgomery, Alabama, sued the newspaper for criticisms in a non-commercial advertisement it published that denounced police tactics used against civil rights demonstrators. Portions of the advertisement included minor factual errors (such as stating that Dr. Martin Luther King had been arrested seven times, when in fact he had been arrested four times). Sullivan claimed that by defaming the police, the newspaper also defamed him because he supervised the police department. He obtained a judgment for presumed and punitive damages of a half-million dollars (in today's dollars, that would be approximately $3.5 million).

The Supreme Court would have none of it, and pruned back the defamation exception to the First Amendment in several respects. First, it rejected the common law's assumption that all false statements should be unprotected. The Court noted that errors are inevitable in debate about public matters, and that a buffer zone to provide "breathing space" for advocacy is needed to encourage people to speak freely. This case provided a very good example, as the false statements were minor mistakes, typical of errors in the newspaper business, and probably never really hurt Commissioner Sullivan's reputation. **The Court ruled that no public official may recover damages for defamation "relating to his official conduct" without proving that the speaker had "actual malice," which the Court defined as**

- **"knowledge that it was false or with**
- **reckless disregard of whether it was false or not."**

This standard reversed the common law requirement that the defendant prove that the criticism was true and also added a requirement that the plaintiff prove the speaker had a culpable state of mind. This created a buffer zone of protection—the speaker's non-reckless belief that the statement was true. **What's the Takeaway? As long as the speaker does not knowingly or recklessly publish harmful falsehoods, the First Amendment denies recovery for defamation of public officials.** The Court's decision tweaked defamation law in other respects, such as clarifying a requirement that the statement defame the plaintiff individually rather than criticize government actions, which was really the case in *Sullivan*. Perhaps most importantly, it underscored the shift in burden of proof, stating that malice must be proved with **"convincing clarity."**

Sullivan ushered in twenty years of active Supreme Court oversight of tort law under the First Amendment. The earliest decisions expanded the scope of the decision. **The malice standard was extended to apply to criticisms of public figures, which has brought celebrities, athletes, entertainers, business leaders, and notorious criminals under the test.** The decision was also interpreted to protect non-reckless falsehoods from other tort claims, such as Infliction of Emotional Harm and the privacy torts. This is why talk show hosts can say outrageous things about politicians and entertainers without facing defamation suits. The television show *South Park* seems to take particular joy in making fun of celebrities and the fact that they are safe from defamation suits. It probably couldn't do so without *New York Times v. Sullivan.*

The Supreme Court began to reverse course about halfway through the twenty-year period. The most important decision was probably *Gertz v. Robert Welch, Inc.* (1974) (Powell), which involved accusations against a Chicago civil rights lawyer who represented the family of an African-American child shot by a Chicago police officer. *American Opinion,* a journal of the right-wing John Birch Society, claimed that Gertz was a Leninist and a member of Marxist organizations. Gertz obtained a libel judgment of $50,000 under the common law rules. The judgment was overturned on the ground that the *New York Times* test should have been used because the underlying issues—the police shooting and racial tensions in the city—were matters of public concern. The appellate court reasoned that the "knowing or reckless disregard" test protects speakers who make understandable factual errors in order to ensure full-scale debate on matters of public concern. The Supreme Court disagreed. **Why?** Private individuals deserve greater protection than public figures receive under defamation law for two reasons. First, public figures have access to the media to present their side of controversial stories, and therefore are not dependent on litigation to protect their reputations. Second, public figures voluntarily give up much of their privacy when they choose to live in the public arena. Thus, **states may allow private individuals to recover for negligently false statements.** The First Amendment still provides some protection in these cases—the common law's strict liability standard and placing the burden of proof on the defendant are not permitted. In addition, in another **Takeaway: punitive damages remain subject to the actual malice test, knowing or reckless falsity.**

The mid-1980s saw a second retreat from the *New York Times* test. In *Dun & Bradstreet, Inc. v. Greenmoss Builders, Inc.* (1985), the Supreme Court considered a case in which Dun & Bradstreet, a credit-reporting agency, included incorrect information that Greenmoss had filed for bankruptcy in reports the agency sent to several customers. Understandably, the inaccurate claim that Greenmoss was in bankruptcy hurt the company's business reputation. A jury awarded compensatory and punitive damages without being instructed on the "actual malice" requirement. The Court upheld the award without a majority opinion, but five justices supported the view that the *Gertz* limitation on punitive damages should not apply in a matter unrelated to the public interest. **The Takeaway? The consensus of a majority of justices was that defamation of a private person (*i.e.* not a public figure) on a wholly private matter should not be subject to the actual malice requirement in any respect.** The Court did not hold that the First Amendment is irrelevant to such private-private defamation—it repeated the caveat that such speech was "not totally unprotected," but provided no more guidance. Lower courts have had little success resolving what protections exist.

So unless your classmate's lab partner is a public official or public figure (both seem unlikely), he or she may have the makings of a good defamation case.

C. Obscenity and Child Pornography

Obscenity is the third traditional exclusion from First Amendment protection. Obscenity has a technical legal meaning far more limited than pornography, even though the terms are often used interchangeably in common English usage. Most pornography is probably protected by the First Amendment. Child pornography, on the other hand, is clearly excluded from First Amendment protection.

As with Incitement and Defamation, Obscenity law evolved in a series of Supreme Court decisions during the 20th century. The Court had a difficult time coming up with a workable test. The best known statement on the subject is by Justice Potter Stewart, who once admitted he couldn't define obscenity but "I know it when I see it." In *Roth v. United States* (1957) (Brennan), the Court focused on looking at the movie or book or magazine (let's just call them "publications") as a whole to determine whether it presents sexual material "in a manner appealing to a prurient interest." (That last part is apparently just legalese for sexually arousing.) Nine years later in *Memoirs v. Massachusetts* (1966) (Brennan), the Court reaffirmed *Roth*, noting that an erotic publication is protected unless it is "patently offensive because it violates contemporary community standards relating to the representation of sex" and "is utterly without redeeming social value." This is a narrow definition, although courts of the era upheld convictions for distributing materials that are now commonplace online.

Miller v. California (1973) (Burger) marked the culmination of this line of cases, as the Court agreed on a test that expanded the exclusion for obscenity. *Miller* set out a deceptively precise three-part test that must be satisfied before a publication may be declared legally obscene (our **Takeaway**):

- "a) whether the **average person**, applying **contemporary community standards**, would find that **the work taken as a whole appeals to the prurient interest;**

- b) whether the work **depicts, in a patently offensive way, sexual conduct specifically defined** by state statute; **and**

- c) whether the work **taken as a whole lacks serious** literary, artistic, political, or scientific **value."**

The biggest problem with this test is that it contains numerous subjective terms, starting with "average person" and ending with "serious . . . value." The Court has acknowledged that each community in which sexually explicit materials are sold could impose its own standards through jury determinations of "prurient interest" under the first part of the test. This alarmed publishers, who feared they would be subject to inconsistent standards because socially conservative communities could be expected to characterize sexually explicit materials as obscene even if they would be tolerated in much of the country. As a practical matter, this would require publishers to limit sexual content to a level that would be acceptable everywhere in the country. Publishers were also concerned with the third part of the test. It abandoned the "utterly without redeeming value" test for what was in essence a judgment call about artistic value (or some other form of merit). Most materials designed for sexual thrills would have to stretch to show an adequate "serious" side under the *Miller* test.

After formulating a comprehensive three-part test in *Miller*, the Supreme Court has been content to leave obscenity cases alone for the most part. Over the years, both the federal government and some states have made occasional efforts to reinvigorate obscenity prosecutions, but have not been very successful, even in communities that would seem receptive to them. Some observers have concluded that most Americans are willing to "live and let live" unless there is evidence of sexual mistreatment. (And it gets even more complicated nowadays, with so much porn and sexually-explicit material on the Internet—see chapter 6.)

In one area, however, states have been aggressive in prosecuting sexually explicit material. In the 1970s, New York enacted a law making it criminal to produce or otherwise promote a "sexual performance" by a child under 16. The Court upheld that law in *New York v. Ferber* (1982) (White). The statutory definition of sexual performance was broad enough to include most visual media of erotic behavior. The term "child pornography" has stuck, and **the definition clearly applies to much more than the "patently offensive" acts of the *Miller* test**, and there is **no exception for works with serious artistic value.** The Court found the purpose of the law was to protect children (the models and actors) from exploitation, rather than to limit permissible reading or viewing content. By punishing any knowing involvement in the distribution of sexually explicit materials involving children, the state could eliminate the commercial trafficking in such materials, which should reduce production of child pornography, and thereby protect a very vulnerable population. This justification outweighed any burden on (arguably) meritorious publications, photographs, or films.

Ferber remains a solid precedent, but one with no apparent application beyond sexual exploitation of juveniles. Attempts to expand *Ferber* to cope with the sexual marketplace on the internet or to justify pornography regulations on protection of women have had little success.

D. Fighting Words, Hate Speech, and True Threats

The last of the traditional categorical exceptions to First Amendment protection is "fighting words." It is arguable that this category is now empty or has morphed into other exceptions, such as "hate speech" or "true threats."

The Fighting Words exception was first recognized by the Supreme Court in *Chaplinsky v. New Hampshire* (1942) (Murphy), in which the Court upheld a conviction for calling a police officer a "God-damned racketeer" and "fascist." Chaplinsky said these things after police responded to complaints that he was publicly and loudly ranting about religion. The Court described **fighting words** as **"those which by their very utterance inflict injury or tend to incite an immediate breach of the peace."** The "<u>or</u>" in this sentence raises an issue. On its face, the first clause seems to mean that many serious insults—those that hurt but aren't likely to elicit any violence—would be sufficient to justify liability. Elsewhere in the opinion, however, the Court emphasized the language after the "or," seeming to limit the definition of fighting words to those that are **likely to result in a violent response**. As such, the Fighting Words doctrine can be seen as a variation on "clear and present danger" in which an *opponent* of the speaker, rather than a *supporter*, is moved to commit an assault or other dangerous act.

Chaplinsky seems quaint today. As a society we tolerate much stronger language, and Court opinions since the 1970s bear that out. *Cohen v. California* (1971) (Harlan) is sometimes seen as overruling *Chaplinsky*, at least in part. In *Cohen*, the Court struck down a Disturbing the Peace conviction of a man who wore a jacket emblazoned with "Fuck the Draft." The Court found no personal provocation in the message, and relied on the marketplace of ideas theory to find a First Amendment value in Cohen's message. We find our **Takeaway** through later decisions that have continued to emphasize *Chaplinsky's* **narrow scope,** striking down convictions while noting that the speech in the case would not precipitate imminent violence, again **in effect using the "clear and present danger" test.**

Two variations of "fighting words" remain credible theories, however. First is the notion that the use of certain words or phrases is **"hate speech,"** words that do nothing but wound (this would be consistent with the language <u>before</u> the "or" in *Chaplinsky*). Two Supreme Court decisions that appear inconsistent with one another are instructive on the difficulties of regulating hate speech. In 1992, the Court struck down a city ordinance that prohibited "fighting words" related to race (as well as to gender and several other categories) in *R.A.V. v. City of St. Paul* (Scalia). A majority concluded that *by selecting only certain fighting words for punishment,* St. Paul discriminated among varieties of speech. Without including all similarly offensive words, the state was making a content-based distinction (*see* chapter 3), thereby violating First Amendment principles that apparently apply even to speech normally excluded from protection. Thus, unless all fighting words— all *hate speech*—are punished, *R.A.V.* seems to rule out punishing hate speech. On the other hand, in *Virginia v. Black* (2003) (O'Connor), the Court upheld Virginia's prohibition of cross-burning where the act is coupled with an intent to intimidate. Since **a burning cross is likely to intimidate and to invite a breach of peace** (either by inciting violence against the victim or provoking the victim to act in self-defense), there is some life in the notion that "fighting words" remain punishable when uttered in a confrontational setting.

The debate about potential First Amendment protection of hate speech remains robust and unresolved. It lives today largely in controversies about university speech codes that prohibit certain language. Many speech codes have been invalidated or rendered ineffective in lower court challenges. Thus, if "fighting words" is to be revitalized as a significant categorical exception to the First Amendment, it may come in a Supreme Court case reviewing a lower court challenge to a speech code. There are also movements to grant states greater authority to regulate hate speech because of the increased use of the internet to bully and harass.

The second variation is rooted in the **"true threat."** If, as *Chaplinsky* suggests, fighting words are verbal provocations that precipitate violence, then punishment seems to be designed to deter violence rather than to punish offensive language. *Virginia v. Black* is consistent with this theory. The Court permitted prosecution of cross-burning *only* where the intent to intimidate was proven. Stated differently, the crime was the combined effect of criminal intent and intimidation of the victim. A classic "fighting words" analysis focuses on the danger of retaliation. Cross-burning or similar intimidation through name-calling or use of symbolic speech (perhaps a simple raised middle finger) fits a contemporary standard for expression that threatens public order, much as the mild epithets deemed unacceptable in the mid-twentieth century justified the ruling in *Chaplinsky*.

So, why do we read and discuss this? While the Supreme Court continues to cite *Chaplinsky*, it may be nothing more than lip service. Those few "fighting words" that remain subject to prosecution are based on conduct, such as intimidation, or some other version of clear and present danger.

Going back to our example of your classmate's posting, we ask whether offensive comments on social media are "fighting words." Possibly (yes, *it depends*). The obstacle would be establishing that they are confrontational because they are not made in the victim's presence, thereby preventing an immediate physical response. That may not matter now that social media is a technological version of "face-to-face." So your classmate *may* have a problem.

E. Commercial Speech

Commercial Speech holds an uncertain place in First Amendment doctrine. It doesn't really belong in this chapter, but it doesn't really belong in any other either. It ends up here primarily because commercial speech was thought to be an exception at one time, and because it provides a good introduction to the Supreme Court's uncertain approaches to speech that is not given full First Amendment protection.

For most of our history, no one really thought of commercial speech as expression protected by the First Amendment. That was probably true of the Congress that proposed the Bill of Rights, as there are no indications society was particularly concerned with a freedom to advertise. As recently as 1994, Justice Scalia argued that commercial speech doctrine should be abandoned in favor of the original meaning from 1791. No one has taken him up on the offer, and even Justice Scalia seems to have concluded that commercial speech is entitled to some constitutional protection.

Instead of an exclusion, commercial speech is simply a second class citizen. Think of regulation of commercial speech as a buffer zone between *speech*, which is generally given broad constitutional protection, and *commercial activity*, which is usually subject to regulation under the rational basis test. **The bottom line—our Takeaway before we have given you case law—for commercial speech is that it is protected by a middle-ground test, something that looks a good bit like the Intermediate Scrutiny that is used in equal protection cases (primarily gender discrimination).**

First, however, we need to figure out what commercial speech is. According to the Supreme Court, it is words (or numbers, photos, symbols) provided as information from a business enterprise to attract purchasers of goods or services. A gas station posts octane numbers and price per gallon. An eBay seller places a violin on auction in a listing that describes the violin, explains its history, sets conditions of sale, and states a starting bid. An auto manufacturer broadcasts a 30 second video of its high performance model driving effortlessly through picturesque mountains. All are examples of commercial speech (short videos even became universally known as "commercials"). Not everything a business enterprise expresses is commercial speech, however. Corporate public affairs offices advocate public policies, such as deregulation and lower business taxes, and do so in a variety of media. A good example is a series of short essays, most on environmental or energy policy, published by ExxonMobil on editorial pages of major newspapers. Such statements are presumably fully protected speech.

The courts first began to recognize First Amendment protection for commercial speech in the 1970s. It was then common for state laws or enforceable ethics codes to prohibit advertising of professional services. The first significant case, *Virginia State Board of Pharmacy v. Virginia Citizens Consumer Council* (1976) (Blackmun), involved a state ban on the advertisement of prescription drug prices. The Court concluded that the interest of consumers in commercial information was comparable to the public interest in political speech. While the Court has backed off from equating political and commercial speech, it has treated commercial speech as entitled to some constitutional protection ever since.

In 1980, the Court decided *Central Hudson Gas & Electric Co. v. Public Service Comm'n* (Powell). The company challenged a Commission ban on promotional advertising, generally defined as advertising products or services that consume energy. The government's rationale was that this regulation would encourage conservation by limiting the market for products that use energy. A majority of the Court adopted a four-part test to analyze laws that limit commercial speech:

- The speech must "concern lawful activity and not be misleading";

- The government must have a "substantial" interest;

- The regulation must "directly advance" that interest;

- The regulation must be no "more extensive than necessary to serve that interest."

The first part of the test is a threshold requirement for the business to gain First Amendment protection. If the speech is about unlawful activity, such as internet advertisements for illegal services, it receives no protection. If the speech is misleading, such as deceptive advertising of diet or health products, it receives no protection. The rest of the test imposes heightened scrutiny. Note that the interest only has to be *substantial*, rather than compelling. Note also that *"directly advances"* is probably closer to Intermediate Scrutiny's "substantially related to" requirement, as opposed to Strict Scrutiny's requirement. The last part, however, looks like a concept you'll see again in this book, a requirement that speech restrictions be no more restrictive than necessary, which seems close to the "necessary" or "narrowly tailored" components of Strict Scrutiny. This test is more than a mouthful, and has been recast somewhat over the years.

While the Court has touched on aspects of the commercial speech doctrine often over the years, sometimes distinguishing or explaining *Central Hudson*, it has never really replaced the case as precedent or the four-part test as governing doctrine. One instructive case is *44 Liquormart v. Rhode Island* (1996). A state law prohibited advertising the price of alcoholic beverages. The nine justices were all over the map. Seven agreed to strike down the law applying the *Central Hudson* test. They split, however, on the meaning of that test. For example, a plurality of four justices concluded that "special care" is needed in reviewing laws that limit the access of consumers to truthful information, and Justice Thomas argued that such laws are *per se* unlawful. That would seem to create a five-justice majority in favor of at least "special care" for truthful commercial speech. On the other hand, seven justices asserted in one way or another that governments retain greater power to regulate commercial speech than other varieties of speech.

The Court has decided several cases that addressed commercial speech since *44 Liquormart*. Those decisions applied the *Central Hudson* test. In each instance the Court struck down or narrowly interpreted commercial speech limitations, generally finding them broader than necessary to achieve the intended purpose. In addition, several justices have left the Court since *44 Liquormart* was decided. None of the recent decisions has required the Court to reconsider doctrine in this area, so the views of nearly half of the justices are unknown.

The Takeaway is the *Central Hudson* **test outlined earlier. Further, and this is more like why we read and discuss these cases, commercial speech remains in an uncertain position, not excluded from protection, but still designated as "lesser" speech.** The more often restrictions are struck down, however, the more it appears that commercial speech may eventually be recognized as fully protected.

F. Additional Categories?

It is unlikely that the Court will establish new categories of excluded expression in the near future, but a couple of areas are worth noting. In *United States v. Stevens* (2010) (Roberts), the Court struck down a federal criminal statute that sought to punish depictions of animal cruelty, apparently in an attempt to criminalize a bizarre and cruel type of animal torture videos called "crush videos" (if you don't already know what they are, trust us, we don't want to explain them). The government argued that because animal cruelty was a well-established crime, and the statute applied only to depictions of illegal acts, the statute served to limit the market for the cruelty videos. This should decrease the supply of the offensive videos, which was essentially the theory the Court accepted in *Ferber,* the child pornography case. Under the government's analysis, a category of speech—here depictions of animal cruelty—could be prohibited because, on balance, the value of the speech (very little if any) was outweighed by the harm to society from the animal cruelty that would exist only because of the commercial market for the videos. The Chief Justice described the government's argument as "startling and dangerous" because it would allow new categories of unprotected speech whenever Congress determines that a type of speech causes more harm than good. His majority opinion limited *Ferber* to its facts, refusing to engage in categorical value balancing.

The Court reached a similar conclusion in *Brown v. Entertainment Merchants Association* (2011) (Scalia), striking down California's law regulating the sale of video games to children based on violent content. California analogized gratuitous violence to obscenity and argued that a new First Amendment categorical exclusion should be created for depictions of violence made available to children. The argument resonates with many people because of their concern that exposure to violence may be even more harmful to children than exposure to offensive sexual images. Still, the Court refused to expand the categories of excluded expression or to redefine obscenity to include violent images, and reviewed California's law under traditional First Amendment principles.

In *Stevens* the Court listed the following categories of unprotected speech: "obscenity, defamation, fraud, incitement, and speech integral to criminal conduct."

Note that this list omits "fighting words," perhaps signaling that this category is in fact no longer recognized, but then adds two new categories to the traditional group. The reason may lie in the word "conduct" in the last category. The words needed to make a crime succeed (speech integral to criminal conduct), from *"let's rob a bank"* to *"stick 'em up,"* are criminal only to the extent they facilitate planned or actual crimes. Similarly, the words used in a fraud scheme are criminal only when coupled with criminal intent and conduct. Fraudulent speech and "speech integral to crime" are "speech," but they may also be evidence of crime. **Nothing in First Amendment case law or theory suggests that protected speech cannot be used as evidence.** A political speech by an officeholder is fully protected by the First Amendment, but may also be evidence of motive or an admission, perhaps in a bribery case. Think of all the stupid things corrupt politicians have said on tape and which were later used against them in criminal cases. Stupid, **yes**, evidence of crime, **yes**, protected by the First Amendment, **also yes**.

Thus, fraud and speech integral to criminal conduct are not really categorical exclusions from the First Amendment, but rather are examples of speech that may be used against the speaker, just like a confession to a police officer (remember the Miranda Warning: "anything you say can be used against you"). This may also explain the place of true threats in First Amendment law. The words alone do not constitute a crime and are not a categorical exception to the First Amendment protection. The *circumstances surrounding their use*, on the other hand, may make them relevant to prove common law crimes, such as assault, and modern statutory offenses, such as Making Terroristic Threats.

Key Takeaway from Chapter 2:

The closing **Takeaway** from this chapter is that there are several traditional First Amendment categorical exclusions: **incitement, defamation, and obscenity (interpreted to include child pornography). Fighting words** may live on as another exclusion for "hate speech" if the courts decide to revitalize the doctrine in that fashion. **Commercial Speech** was once an exception, and now lives as a "second tier" right, although the trend of the Supreme Court has been to strike down most limits on truthful commercial speech.

———————

THINGS TO KNOW

- Clear and Present Danger (incitement)

- The actual malice requirement—knowledge or reckless disregard (defamation)

- The negligence standard for private individuals (defamation)

- You may not need to memorize the *Miller* test, but you should at least focus on these things, all of which must be proven to convict in an obscenity case:

  o   the work as a whole

  o   community standards

  o   patently offensive sexual conduct

  o   lack of serious value

- And then pat yourself on the back because you just did better than Justice Stewart.

- Fighting words—The "likely to cause a breach of the peace" standard remains law, even if fewer words have this effect today.

- Untruthful commercial speech is not protected.

- Truthful commercial speech is subject to a test that in practice is quite protective.

- The Supreme Court is reluctant to add to exclusions from First Amendment protection.

THINGS TO THINK ABOUT

- The "shouting fire" analogy

- The Marketplace of Ideas

- Are there other ways to protect the reputations of public officials and public figures?

- *Miller* was seen as a victory for opponents of obscene materials. So why are there so few obscenity prosecutions? Is it that society has been coarsened by pervasive sexual images? Is it tolerance for something many see as victimless (rightly or wrongly)?

- Hate speech can be truly despicable. In recent years the Supreme Court has held its nine noses and struck down restrictions on *very* offensive statements. Where should it draw the line and why?

- Does the Supreme Court's inclusion of fraud and "speech integral" to crime make sense as exclusions under the First Amendment? Perhaps there are other exclusions we just don't think about in those terms. If so, why not add depictions of animal cruelty and violent images in video games to the excluded categories?

CHAPTER 3

How Government Restricts Speech

Broadly speaking, we do not want the government to prohibit speech *based on its content*. Today, the Court has settled on an analytical framework that focuses on questions of content-neutrality. When the government regulates speech based on content, as a general rule the First Amendment dictates that courts must apply Strict Scrutiny. As you may recall from Con Law, Strict Scrutiny analysis generally requires the government to prove that a law is necessary to achieve a compelling governmental interest, usually in least restrictive or intrusive means available. *Government regulations which are content-based are presumptively invalid, while those which are content-neutral are not. Even when the government seeks to regulate speech in a content-neutral fashion, the Court imposes a heavy burden upon the government.*

A. Content-Based/Content-Neutral Regulations

This chapter looks at questions of how the government regulates speech, and corresponding issues of levels of scrutiny. The scrutiny questions build on the basic tiers of scrutiny analysis you encountered in Con Law. As a quick reminder for context, Equal Protection analysis employs three tiers: Strict Scrutiny, Intermediate Scrutiny, and Rational Basis review. When analyzing fundamental rights, such as speech rights, courts employ Strict Scrutiny.

How does **Strict Scrutiny** apply in the First Amendment context? When the government seeks to regulate expressive content, the court imposes a heavy burden of justification, making the law presumptively invalid. *Strict Scrutiny requires government to prove that the law is necessary to achieve a compelling interest.* Why? This helps prevent censorship, or protecting against our fear of government targeting messages it does not like. In its 1994 decision in *Turner Broadcasting System v. FCC*, the Court said that regulation of speech "pose[s] the inherent risk that the Government seeks not to advance a legitimate regulatory goal, but to suppress unpopular ideas or information or to manipulate the public debate through coercion rather than persuasion. We employ Strict Scrutiny so as to make sure the government is not trying to silence views solely on the basis of the opinion being expressed." With that backdrop, we now look at how speech regulations are analyzed.

Content- and Subject-Neutrality: The core concept behind First Amendment protection against the government shutting down unpopular ideas or points of view is *content-* or *viewpoint-neutrality*. The state cannot single out and censor speech based on its content or point-of-view. The government also may not censor based on subject matter; that is known as *subject*-neutrality, and that also serves key First Amendment goals. In numerous cases, the Court has maintained its Strict Scrutiny of subject matter restrictions, because if the government can target particular subjects, it can distort the marketplace of ideas just as much as the suppression of particular viewpoints. So, for example, if there is an unpopular war, a restriction on discussing the *subject* of the war could have nearly the same dangerous impact as a ban that prohibited people from expressing their *view* that the war is wrong. The subject-matter restriction could effectively shut down the dissenters, and their point of view.

With that introduction, we explore various ways in which the government restricts speech, and the Court's reaction to those limits. First, we examine *Content-Neutral Laws and Symbolic Conduct*. This stems from a key question about when conduct becomes speech. Activities—marches, pickets, cross-burning—and things—armbands, jackets—are symbolic and carry messages. The Court has consistently treated symbolic conduct (and effects) as speech deserving First Amendment protection. But what are the limits? Our key inquiry is: *When should conduct be analyzed as speech; and when we do treat conduct as speech, how do we analyze?*

Our analysis starts with the 1968 decision in *United States v. O'Brien* (Warren). The case involved a man who had been convicted for burning his draft card, as part of a symbolic protest against the Vietnam War. He undeniably violated a federal law which prohibited the knowing destruction or mutilation of draft cards. Many had seen this law as a way to curb Vietnam War protests. O'Brien saw this law, and his conviction, as an inappropriate restriction on his expressive rights, protected by the First Amendment. The Court addressed the central issue of how to sort out conduct and speech, when they are intertwined, writing: "when 'speech' and 'nonspeech' elements are combined in the same course of conduct, a sufficiently important governmental interest in regulating the nonspeech element can justify incidental limits on First Amendment freedoms." In other words, sometimes regulating *conduct* has a connected impact on speech; if so, the conduct restriction may survive judicial scrutiny, despite the otherwise disfavored limit on the expressive element. The Court set forth a test to evaluate communicative conduct, holding that a regulation may be justified if:

- it is within the government's constitutional power;

- it furthers an important or substantial governmental interest;

- the governmental interest is *unrelated* to the suppression of free expression; and

- the incidental restriction on First Amendment freedom is no greater than essential to furtherance of interest.

The Court applied this test to the law at hand and upheld it as constitutional. **Do you agree? Why (not)?**

What's the Takeaway? In this context, there is a clear ban on expressive conduct, but it still survived Court scrutiny, under the test above. No speech is absolutely protected. The government can regulate conduct that communicates if it has an important interest unrelated to the suppression of the message and if the impact on expression is no more than necessary to achieve the governmental goal. (That sounds a lot like *Intermediate Scrutiny*.) The Court's four-part test controls situations where restrictions on expressive conduct restrict free expression.

The Court applied the *O'Brien* test to a flag desecration statute in the 1989 *Texas v. Johnson* case (Brennan) that drew much attention in the general public. In that case, Johnson participated in a public demonstration outside the Republican Convention in Dallas, burning a flag and chanting "America, the red, white, and blue, we spit on you." He was using both his conduct (flag burning) and words (chanting) to express his objections to Pres. Reagan and the Republican Party. The Court saw the flag burning as protected expressive conduct and applied *O'Brien*. To the extent that the State of Texas argued that its law was in part designed to prevent a breach of peace, the Court rejected that concern, as there was no breach—it was a peaceful protest. In addition, Texas had expressed an interest in protecting the flag as a symbol of nationhood and national unity. The Court found that to be improperly related to suppressing expression. Applying *O'Brien,* the Court held that the regulation was directly related to suppressing a particular form of expression and failed the third part of the test. The Court observed: "If there is a bedrock principle underlying the First Amendment, it is that the Government may not prohibit the expression of an idea simply because society finds the idea itself offensive or disagreeable." And that was the case in *Texas v. Johnson*—the government did not like the message conveyed by the flag-burning. The ultimate irony of the law (and the opinion) was expressed as follows: "We do not consecrate the flag by punishing its desecration, for in doing so we dilute the freedom that this cherished emblem represents." In an emotional dissent, Chief Justice Rehnquist argued that "Flag burning is the equivalent of an inarticulate grunt or roar that is most likely to be indulged in not to express any particular idea, but to antagonize others." He saw the ban as more appropriately seen as a way to prevent fights, but not as an inappropriate limit of expressive conduct.

What's the Takeaway? In directly regulating *conduct*, the state *indirectly* may be limiting expressive activity, protected by the First Amendment. In this context, the government cannot ban flag burning, even though—and maybe particularly because— it is highly expressive and emotional.

Why do we read and discuss these cases? These opinions show us that the government often regulates conduct, but in areas and in ways that have a significant impact on expressive activity. Sometimes, the government is trying to regulate permissibly, within a sphere in its domain, but other times the regulation is a thinly-veiled attempt to stifle unpopular messages. Thus while the regulation is content-neutral, in fact it is intended to suppress one perspective and elevate a competing one. Whether this is permissible depends on the outcome of the *O'Brien* test. The First Amendment and *O'Brien* protects against government attempts to suppress unpopular, controversial, or divergent speech.

The Court more recently ruled on content-based vs. content-neutral restrictions on First Amendment activity in its 2010 decision in *Holder v. Humanitarian Law Project* (Roberts). The case considered a challenge to a federal statute, Title 18 U.S.C. § 2339B, which criminalizes knowingly providing any material support or resources to foreign terrorist organizations. Congress' definition of "material support or resources" included examples such as currency, training, and expert advice or assistance. Two U.S. citizens and six domestic organizations challenged the law, because they wanted to provide money, legal training, and political advocacy to the Partiya Karkeran Kurdistan (PKK) and the Liberation Tigers of Tamil Eelam (LTTE) in order to support their humanitarian and political purposes. PKK and LTTE were both designated as foreign terrorist organizations because of evidence that they committed numerous terrorist attacks and have harmed American citizens. The Court thus considered whether the material support statute violates the plaintiffs' First Amendment rights to freedom of speech and association because it does not require the government to prove that plaintiffs had specific intent to further the terrorist organization's illegal activities.

The Court found the statute to be constitutional *as applied*, holding that it did not violate the plaintiffs' freedom of speech because even providing terrorist organizations support for lawful, nonviolent purposes can bolster terrorist activities. The majority applied a "more demanding standard" than Intermediate Scrutiny because the statute was seen to be a *content-based* regulation of speech since "[p]laintiffs want to speak to the PKK and the LTTE, and whether they may do so under § 2339B depends on what they say." Thus, this fell outside of *O'Brien* and demanded strict scrutiny. "The law here may be described as directed at conduct, . . . but as applied to plaintiffs the conduct triggering coverage under the statute consists of communicating a message". **What's the Takeaway?** Applying heightened scrutiny, the Court held that the government has a compelling interest in preventing terrorism and banning material support and services to terrorist organization is necessary to further that interest.

Why do we read and discuss this case? The *Humanitarian Law Project* case shows that while the *O'Brien* test still applies to some cases, there is a fine line to walk, and this case crossed one key line. While the statute in question addresses specific conduct, it still is targeted at certain points of view. It thus was not seen as *content-neutral*, but rather as *content-based*, demanding Strict Scrutiny. Nonetheless, the Court was somewhat deferential to the executive branch in finding that the statute as applied was necessary to fulfill a compelling government interest.

B. Time, Place & Manner Regulations

The government maintains a significant power to regulate expressive activities *indirectly*. The state also sometimes *directly* regulates speech activities, in terms of the time, place, and manner of the activity. Where, when and how loudly you speak and the like are known as *time place and manner* restrictions on speech. There's no question that the government is directly targeting the speech activity in question, but it is *not* directly concerned with the content of the speech. *If* there's a good reason, the Court will tolerate many such regulations.

For example, we don't allow for people to blast music as loud as they want at all hours of the day and night. Except perhaps Lloyd Dobler, played by John Cusack in *Say Anything*, or Radio Raheem in

Do the Right Thing, two movie classics from 1989 (ask your parents). Both these characters are famous for playing their boom boxes, at their chosen volume, and getting plenty of attention. We instinctively know that you have to keep the volume down, because (1) it bothers other people, and (2) if everybody played their music as loud as they wanted, we would all be washed away in an impossible sea of noise. So we allow regulation. The key questions we explore in this analysis go to whether the regulation in question is really targeted to the expression itself, or just the time, place, and manner. For that reason we still rely on the same basic concepts of neutrality—the more it is based on content or viewpoint, the more suspect a regulation becomes.

In *Ward v. Rock Against Racism* (1989) (Kennedy) the Court upheld a regulation that required concerts in a bandshell in a public park to keep volume at or below certain levels, and for the band to use amplification equipment and a technician provided by the city. The Court held: "a regulation of the time, place, or manner of protected speech must be narrowly tailored to serve the government's legitimate, content-neutral interests but that it need not be the least restrictive or least intrusive means of doing so. Rather, the requirement of narrow tailoring is satisfied 'so long as the . . . regulation promotes a substantial government interest that would be achieved less effectively absent the regulation.' To be sure, this standard does not mean that a time, place, or manner regulation may burden substantially more speech than is necessary to further the government's legitimate interests. . . . So long as the means chosen are not substantially broader than necessary to achieve the government's interest, however, the regulation will not be invalid simply because a court concludes that the government's interest could be adequately served by some less-speech-restrictive alternative."

Forum analysis presents the question of *where* the speech is taking place. While content-based regulation of protected speech in a public forum is subject to Strict Scrutiny, content-neutral regulations which indirectly burden speech do not have to meet the same burden. Time, place, and manner regulation of the *context* in which speech occurs should be content-neutral and is subject to a lower level of scrutiny. The degree of judicial scrutiny will often turn on the nature of the public place being regulated—**traditional public forum, limited or designated public forum, or nonpublic forum.**

Speech is most protected in a *public forum*. This is the kind of place most naturally associated with the notion of the street-corner speaker or one in a public park, perhaps standing on a soap-box, shouting to gathered onlookers and passers-by, about the key issues of the day. It's an old-fashioned (outdated?) idea, but one worth remembering. As we discussed in the introductory chapter, the First Amendment plays a crucial role in allowing for a robust wide-open public debate on important issues of the day. And such a discussion requires a *place* to be had. While in today's society so much more conversation takes place virtually, there is still no way to replace an in-person speech, debate or dialog. As a result, we still see vigorous protection for the time-honored public forum.

Early public forum cases establish the key principle that some places must be held out and protected for people to engage in public debate. In a 1939 Supreme Court decision, *Hague v. C.I.O.*, the Court overturned a ban on political meetings in public places. The Court relied on the concept that public property has an historic function in the promotion of First Amendment ideals: "Wherever the title of streets and parks may rest, they have immemorially been held in trust for the use of the public and, time out of mind, have been used for purposes of assembly, communicating thoughts between citizens, and discussing public questions. Such use of the streets and public places has, from ancient times, been a part of the privileges, immunities, rights, and liberties of citizens. The privilege of a citizen of the United States to use the streets and parks for communication of views on national questions may be regulated in the interest of all; it is not absolute, but relative, and must be exercised in subordination to the general comfort and convenience, and in consonance with peace and good order; but it must not, in the guise of regulation, be abridged or denied." Thus the Court guaranteed access to certain areas, for purposes of speech.

Later that year, in *Schneider v. State* (Roberts) the Court reviewed a series of municipal ordinances that prohibited passing out leaflets (and other expressive activities) on public streets, arguably to prevent litter and maintain a clean and safe public streetscape. In its analysis the Court stressed the need to balance legitimate competing interests, but noted that it must be done carefully. **"This constitutional protection does not deprive a city of all power to prevent street littering. There are obvious methods to prevent street littering."** If the law indirectly or incidentally burdens freedom of speech, the Court will likely engage in some form of balancing to determine if the law is reasonable, weighing the interests of the government in regulating the activity against the burden on free speech interests. The state has the power to regulate, but the ordinances in question went too far. Also, the Court acknowledged that the analysis must recognize the scarcity of opportunities available to distribute messages, and the meaningfulness of certain forums. "The streets are natural and proper places for the dissemination of information and opinion; and one is not to have the exercise of his liberty of expression in appropriate places abridged on the plea that it may be exercised in some other place." In so doing, the Court importantly ruled that access alone is not enough. The speaker must have some sort of *meaningful* access to a public forum. It's somewhat like the age-old question: *If a tree falls in a forest and nobody is around to hear it, does it make a sound?*

What's the Takeaway? It's a matter of **tailoring and balancing and deference.** The Court explores the way the government chooses to regulate, balancing the government's legitimate interests against the burdens on speech. The more closely tailored to fit the government need, the more likely the regulation will stand. That analysis also raises questions of deference that crop up throughout the book—the more deferential courts are to government, the more likely the restriction on expressive activity is to stand.

In *Clark v. Community for Creative Non-Violence* (1984) (White), the National Park Service issued a permit to Community for Creative Non-Violence (CCNV) to conduct a winter demonstration in Lafayette Park, across the street from the White House, to bring attention to the plight of the homeless. The permit allowed CCNV to put up twenty tents in the park. But federal regulations only permitted camping in National Parks in *campgrounds* designated for that purpose, which did not include Lafayette Park. Importantly, the definition of camping in the regulation includes "the use of park land for living accommodation purposes such as sleeping activities." As a result, the Park Service denied CCNV's request to allow the demonstrators to *sleep* in the tents. CCNV challenged this denial.

While keeping the park open for expressive activity and protest, the Court rejected CCNV's argument. The Court held that the regulation prohibiting demonstrators from sleeping in the tents for their demonstration did not violate the First Amendment. The park was still open for some expressive activity; and the government had a good, content-neutral, reason to restrict activity. In an extension of *O'Brien*, the Court found this regulation to be a content-neutral requirement since the demonstrators were not prohibited from sleeping at the parks *because of* their message about the plight of the homeless. The government's significant interest for the regulation is to maintain the parks near the White House in a condition that would continue to attract millions of people who want to enjoy them. That interest was held to be unrelated the suppression of expression, and the Court found that the demonstrators were still able to convey their message through the tents in the park and signs.

What's the Takeaway? Time, place, and manner restrictions are valid, "provided they are justified without reference to the content of the regulated speech, that they are narrowly tailored to serve a significant governmental interest, and that they leave open ample alternative channels for communication of the information." This last part is also key to our broader understanding of our subject; the First Amendment guarantees some access to a forum, or an alternative way for a speaker to get her message out.

A very recent Supreme Court case involving abortion clinic protest buffer zones builds on these concepts. In *McCullen v. Coakley* (2014) (Roberts) the Court reviewed the Massachusetts Reproductive Health Care Facilities Act, which criminalized knowingly standing within 35 feet of any reproductive health care facility where abortions are performed, other than a hospital. The Act exempted four classes of people, including employees of the facility acting within their scope of employment. The statute was challenged by individuals who engaged in "sidewalk counseling" at health care facilities that provide abortion, where they would approach women walking into to the facility to offer them information about alternative options. They argued that the buffer zones significantly hindered their efforts by limiting their ability to initiate up-close, personal conversations in public places. Their efforts were also frustrated because escorts would accompany patients through the buffer zones, which they were allowed to do since the Act had an exemption for such employees. The Court applied *CCNV* to this situation, holding that while the Government's ability to limit speech in public places is limited, it can impose reasonable restrictions on the time, place, or manner of speech. Those restrictions may survive heightened scrutiny, if they are "justified without reference to the content of the regulated speech, that they are narrowly tailored to serve a significant governmental interest, and that they leave open ample alternative channels for communication of the information." While regulation *may* be possible, the Court stated the standard as follows: "To meet the requirement of narrow tailoring, the government must demonstrate that alternative measures that burden substantially less speech would fail to achieve the government's interests, not simply that the chosen route is easier." The Court found the law in this case not to be narrowly tailored because Massachusetts did not explore less burdensome methods that were effective in other jurisdictions.

What's the Takeaway? The Court held that some form of heightened scrutiny applies to this situation: "We must ask whether the challenged provisions of the injunction burden no more speech than necessary to serve a significant government interest." While this seems to be slightly more deferential to the government than traditional Strict Scrutiny, the Court ruled that the government overstepped its bounds.

Why do we read and discuss these cases? This goes back to the concepts of tailoring, balancing and deference. *CCNV* shows the Court's **deference to authorities** even when employing heightened scrutiny to speech restrictions (*a recurring theme*). These cases also force us to consider how much the message is entwined with the medium and mode of expression. As Justice Marshall argued in dissent in *CCNV*, content-neutral regulations can unnecessarily restrict protected First Amendment activity, where the acts are an essential part of the expression. In that context he argued that sleep was integral to the demonstration because it is part of the reality for homeless people who have to sleep outside in the winter. While the majority rejected that argument, you should be able to see that regulating conduct could easily encroach on expressive activities. Reaching a contrary result, the Court in *McCullen v. Coakley* struck down the restrictions in question, showing less deference to government regulations. There, the majority was more sympathetic to the protestors, and found that the restrictions were too burdensome on speech activities. In both cases, cutting two different ways, the *conduct* is often the message, or fully intertwined with it. The deference or lack thereof is instructive and leads to a question as to whether this may be results-oriented jurisprudence. One recent study showed that, as a general matter, the current Justices more often rule with speech with which they agree, ideologically speaking. "While liberal justices are over all more supportive of free speech claims than conservative justices, . . . the votes of both liberal and conservative justices tend to reflect their preferences toward the ideological groupings of the speaker." This is consistent with studies over the years which show what is often called an "in-group bias". Judges are human after all. **Do you think that there is a results-oriented skew, based on ideology?**

Why else do we read and discuss these cases? They go to the heart of the analytical challenge, which is present throughout all individual rights cases, and our context of First Amendment analysis. The key question here is: *How do we strike the right balance between governmental interests and individual rights?* Litter vs. Order. Noise vs. Tranquility. Visual Blight vs. Cleanliness. Expression vs. Silence. We must consistently ensure that the government is not targeting the *content*, and instead only acting within its proper sphere of regulation. Prohibiting litter is fine. Banning leaflets that address political issues, or challenge the government, is not. It is fine to stop people from blaring sound all day and night, but it is not permissible to stop people from speaking above a barely audible whisper. It is especially problematic to limit volume when the motivation is based on the *content* or the *message*. What are the limits? The state may limit speaking time to ensure that all get a chance to speak and be heard, but *not* in order to squelch opinion or opposition.

These concepts also predominate when talking about *where* speech may occur, when not in a park, on the sidewalk, or similarly traditional forums. While the Court has consistently held that places like public parks and streets are to be held out for the exchange of ideas (subject to limitations, as we just discussed), what do we do in other settings? Additional case law deals with locations *other than* traditional public forums.

Perry Education Association v. Perry Local Educators' Association (White) dealt with this in a school setting in 1983. The case name itself is tricky enough, and it involved two rival organizations that represented teachers in a school district. The PEA had been elected to have exclusive bargaining representation rights for the teachers. PLEA, its rival, wanted access to the members on equal terms as PEA. Specifically, PEA had rights to use in-school mailboxes, to which PLEA wanted access. The question became whether the in-school mailboxes were a public forum to which both organizations must have equal access.

The Court held that the mailboxes were a *nonpublic forum,* the Justices further found no evidence of an improper intent to suppress or promote any particular viewpoint. That allowed limits on PLEA access to the mailboxes. In a nonpublic forum, speech rights are less expansive than in a traditional public forum. Justice White wrote: "Implicit in the concept of the nonpublic forum is the right to make distinctions in access on the basis of subject matter and speaker identity. These distinctions may be impermissible in a public forum but are inherent and inescapable in the process of limiting a nonpublic forum to activities compatible with the intended purpose of the property. The touchstone for evaluating these distinctions is whether they are reasonable in light of the purpose which the forum at issue serves." Because there was no policy of unrestricted public access to the mailboxes, and because the selective policy did not render them open to general public, the Court ruled that these were *limited public forums* at best. Additionally, because PLEA had *alternative avenues* for communicating with teachers, the Court was convinced that limiting mailbox access to PEA was constitutional. The dissent saw this as failing strict scrutiny, as no other group besides PLEA was actually being excluded from this channel of communication. This case seems to hinge in part on questions of whether the outward intent was to discriminate (which the majority said it was not), or whether the impact was to exclude, based on point-of-view (which the dissent argued is central).

Members of City Council v. Taxpayers for Vincent (1984) (Stevens) raises the issues of *Schneider* (the 1939 leafletting case) again. Specifically, *Vincent* involved signs posted on public property—utility poles. Here the Court held that the "substantive evil—visual blight . . . is created by the medium of expression itself." The majority wrote "a restriction on expressive activity may be invalid if the remaining modes of communication are inadequate." But having said that, the majority concluded that "there are ample alternative modes of communication in Los Angeles."

Likewise in *Cornelius v. NAACP Legal Defense and Educational Fund* (1985) (O'Connor) the Court explored the nonpublic forum issue, this time in the context of charitable giving by federal employees. In this case, certain groups were excluded from participating in the Combined Federal Campaign, an annual charity fund drive conducted by the federal government, to which federal employees could donate. The Court saw this as involving protected speech in a nonpublic forum. From that starting point, the opinion provides a good summary of the analytical framework. In terms of nonpublic forum analysis, the Court concluded that there is *not* "a requirement that the restriction be narrowly tailored or that the Government's interest be compelling. The First Amendment does not demand unrestricted access to a nonpublic forum merely because use of that forum may be the most efficient means of delivering the speaker's message." Applying their rule to the facts, the Court also said that the restriction seemed acceptable, in large part because the Justices discerned no ill motive.

In *International Society for Krishna Consciousness (ISKCon) v. Lee* (1992) (Rehnquist), the Court considered regulations by the Port Authority of New York and New Jersey, a joint agency of the two states. The regulations banned repetitive requests for donations and all leafletting in the terminal areas of the Port Authority's three airports. (Note the date—well before the events of 9-11 ushered in the airports we know today.) The plaintiff was the religion commonly known as Hari Krishna, which was notorious for aggressive panhandling and leafletting (and for colorful outfits and interminable chanting). ISKCon challenged the regulations as invading the First Amendment rights of its members by imposing unjustified speech regulations in a public forum, the concourses of the terminals that are open to the public.

A closely-divided Supreme Court upheld the solicitation ban but rejected the leafletting ban. A majority concluded that airports are not public forums. Chief Justice Rehnquist's opinion relied heavily on the earlier cases that recognized that one attribute of a traditional public forum is a long history of use of the property for public debate. Airports are too new to have a long history of such use, and therefore cannot qualify as public forums. The unstated message is that there probably won't be any new public forums recognized because one requirement for recognition is that public forum status has long been recognized. This is like the old law school joke: the Federal Courts course is so hard it should be open only to students who have already taken it. So treat this category as pretty much closed. Of course, designated public forums can always be created, so keep an eye out for governments that provide rooms or other opportunities for public discourse and debate in public buildings.

The distinction between a public forum and a non-public forum made a big difference in the *ISKCon* case. The solicitation ban was upheld because it was generally reasonable, as is required for a non-public forum. Repetitive requests for cash are likely to be disruptive and may lead to something like extortion in busy, fast moving places such as airports. The leafletting ban was struck down, on the other hand, because four justices who favored using the more rigorous public forum test joined with Justice O'Connor, who felt the leafletting ban was not even generally reasonable. Leafletting is a traditional method of expression and unlikely to obstruct airport activities. Thus, prohibiting leafletting could not withstand the more rigorous review applicable to public forums, and may not even be generally reasonable.

What's the Takeaway? In a nonpublic forum, courts will apply something less than strict scrutiny analysis; in doing so, one major concern will be the government's motive in regulating. As noted in *Clark* the key issue is "whether [regulations] are reasonable in light of the purpose which the forum at issue serves." *Vincent* adds a point of emphasis of the importance of alternative channels/avenues of communication.

Why do we read and discuss these cases? The Court is not just looking at the question of how speech is regulated, based on the nature of the forum. Beyond that, the Court appears to be elevating the principle of viewpoint-neutrality, allowing for limited access to a (nonpublic) forum, as long as specific perspectives are not being singled out based on their message. The government motive is a major concern, perhaps more than access to the place being regulated. But by using the nonpublic forum label, the Court avoids harder questions and closer scrutiny.

C. Secondary Effects

We look at one last way in which expressive conduct may be restricted in a way that may seem content-based. But of course it would be improper for the government to restrict speech based on its content. Right? The Court has held that if the law is targeted at other concerns, not the objectionable content, then the government may regulate. When certain *conduct* is targeted, while the government may not regulate based on content, it may do so in order to address the **secondary effects** of the expressive activity. What does that mean? A couple of quick examples, involving regulation of sexually-explicit expressive activity, illustrate.

While "exotic" or "erotic" dancing is partly protected expression, the Court has held that municipalities still may regulate such expressive conduct under a secondary effects analysis. The government cannot regulate solely because it objects to the expression itself, but it may regulate things like related criminal activity that may occur near a topless bar, for example. In the 1986 case of *Renton v. Playtime Theatres* (Rehnquist), an adult movie theater challenged a city zoning ordinance that prohibited adult motion picture theaters from locating within 1,000 feet of any residential zone, single- or multiple-family dwelling, church, park, or school. Movie theater owners accurately argued that adult movies cannot be banned outright due to objections over their content. Nonetheless, the Court held that the ordinance did not improperly restrict First Amendment rights because it was *content-neutral* and necessary to prevent the *secondary effects* of such theaters. The law was backed up with a study that addressed crime patterns in and around such businesses. The central concept was that the ordinance did not ban the theaters altogether, but merely provided where such theaters could (and could not) be located. If the city only was targeting crime, not speech, then *that* regulation might escape the same stringent First Amendment scrutiny. With the city having a substantial interest in regulating the secondary effects of such theaters, the Court held it was a permissible time, place, and manner regulation.

In the 2002 decision in *Los Angeles v. Alameda Books* (O'Connor), the Court affirmed the central holding of *Renton*, upholding the city's zoning ordinances, based on concerns for the secondary effects of the locations of adult book stores. The Court reaffirmed that crimes like prostitution, drug transactions, and petty crimes decreased under these zoning laws. The law in *Alameda Books* was upheld as a proper time, place, and manner restriction motivated by a desire to reduce these unwanted secondary effects, not intended to squelch expressive activity itself, based on its content or message.

What's the Takeaway? Municipalities may not regulate adult movie theaters, book stores etc., solely because of a dislike of the content of the movies shown and books and magazines sold. But they may regulate *if* the target of the regulation is the secondary effects, such as reducing prostitution, drug sales, sexual assaults and the like.

Why do we read these cases? While the true purpose may be to regulate the pornography business, which would be unconstitutional content-based regulation, this analytical framework allows the laws to stand. In that sense, it almost seems like an end-run around the First Amendment analysis, as long as the municipality provides the proper evidence to support its content-neutral decision. Reviewing courts look at secondary effects, and in doing so they avoid the thornier question about content-based suppression of speech activities.

THINGS TO KNOW

- Government action that regulates expression based on its content must satisfy Strict Scrutiny.

- Content-neutral regulations (of Time, Place, or Manner) are subject to a test much like Intermediate Scrutiny in operation. The law must directly promote a substantial government interest and leave open adequate opportunities for speakers to get their message to interested listeners.

- Learn the various categories of forum analysis: traditional public forum, designated public forum, limited public forum, non-public forum, and the appropriate standard of review for each.

- Recognize when government is regulating the secondary effects of expression, such as criminal activity associated with pornographic video stores, as courts are more deferential to government regulation that limits speech than in most other settings.

THINGS TO THINK ABOUT

- When is conduct treated as speech?

- Why are content-neutral regulations given more deference than content-based regulations, at least where the same speech or expression is banned or punished?

- What about laws that are intended to prevent certain communications—like counseling against abortion—but are on their face "content neutral"? Does this explain some seemingly inconsistent results in cases dealing with picketing or other forms of protest?

CHAPTER 4

Government in
Special Roles

Government doesn't always "govern." For example, very often it acts as an employer or property owner. Perhaps a law firm fired one of your friends for wearing a political campaign button at work. This happened soon after her apartment complex refused to renew her lease because she held Tea Party meetings there. The state action rule means that *private* employers and property owners can usually "abridge" speech in this fashion.

May the government abridge speech in similar situations? The Constitution definitely applies when government acts as *the state*— regulating and taxing the public for the common good. But governments also employ millions of people and own vast tracts of property. Do they act subject to the strict limitations of the First Amendment when they fill such roles? The answer, unsurprisingly, is *sometimes,* or *it depends.* Government acts subject to the First Amendment at some level simply because *it still is government.* But the restrictions are looser with respect to an employer's interest in controlling communications by its agents and a landlord's interest in the use of its property.

This chapter examines government power to regulate speech in these two central areas: 1) speech by government employees, and 2) speech on government property. It then takes short, and necessarily somewhat simplistic snapshots of two other areas: public education and spending.

A. Public Employees

Government employment is one of the most common battlegrounds of free speech litigation. To what extent are government employees free to say controversial (or even stupid) things without fear of being disciplined or even fired? From a different angle, to what extent may a government agency insist that its employees *not* make certain statements? The instinctive answer may shift depending on how the issue is phrased. When the focus is on the individual's expression, the tendency is to treat employee freedom to speak as a default setting. When the focus turns to the fact that employers have strong interests in many of the things their employees say, there is a natural inclination to look for limits on freedom of speech. **One early Takeaway that can be drawn from the Supreme Court's case law is that speech by a government employee made in a private capacity is presumably protected, but that speech made in an official action is presumptively, perhaps definitively, unprotected.** Using this test is better than a coin toss on a multiple choice question, but not by very much. For an essay, your go-to can be interest balancing and comparing the value of the private speech to the countervailing government interests.

If you have time to dig deeper, however, you will need to trace the Supreme Court's path. That begins in 1968, when the Court decided *Pickering v. Board of Education* (Marshall) in favor of a teacher who was fired after writing a letter that was critical of certain school board policies to a local newspaper. The Court seemed to have little difficulty finding the appropriate balance in this setting. School board policies are matters of public concern, and a schoolteacher brings interest and special insight to the subject. The speech served free expression values, and the school board made no showing that submitting the letter had adversely affected the teacher's performance in the classroom. The opinion suggests a fairly broad case-by-case balancing approach, in which the government employer would have to prove an adverse effect on the workplace in order to prevail. As long as the subject of the expression fit within the general concept of "public interest," the burden would fall on the employer.

Some later cases, however, have been less "speech-friendly." The case that dominated the area for many years, *Connick v. Myers* (1982) (White), seemed to put the burden on the employee. Harry Connick, *Senior* was the District Attorney of New Orleans (fun fact: his son, Harry Connick, *Junior*, is a singer, actor, and American Idol judge), and Myers was an Assistant District Attorney. Connick fired Myers for distributing a questionnaire among office attorneys, which sought opinions on a number of administrative policies, the merits of supervisors, and perceptions that the assistants were pressured to work on political campaigns. The Supreme Court declared that most of Myers' questionnaire (the speech at issue) was not a matter of public concern, and was therefore wholly outside any free speech protection. This suggested a threshold obstacle for employees making a free speech claim: ***Unless the speech is on a matter of public concern, the First Amendment does not protect speech by government employees***. The political campaign issue, on the other hand, did qualify as a matter of public concern, and therefore the Court applied the *Pickering* balancing test to this part of the questionnaire. Unfortunately for Myers, the Court concluded that the adverse effects of the implied criticisms of internal office policies—the *non*-First Amendment bulk of her questionnaire—outweighed the public interest in the political campaign issues and justified her firing. One can easily pick at *Connick*'s reasoning, questioning, for example, why ineffective or unfair management and personnel policies in a public law office are not matters of public concern. The opinion can also be read to suggest that the Court just took Connick's word (raising issues of *deference*) that the questionnaire damaged workplace relations (apparently more than firing someone for asking the questions in the first place, a dubious proposition). If so, this would seem to place a fairly severe burden on speech.

The Court again reviewed District Attorney/Assistant D.A. relations in *Garcetti v. Ceballos* (2006) (Kennedy). Assistant District Attorney Ceballos was disciplined for writing an internal memo complaining about police misconduct in submitting search warrant applications to the office. The Court declined to apply the *Pickering* balancing test. The memo was written in the course of Ceballos's official duties—by definition, it was *not* speech in a private capacity. Yet, lying by police officers would still seem to be a "matter of public concern."

This emphasizes an important aspect of employee speech rights—the format of the communication, not the importance of the subject matter, may determine whether the balancing test is applied. On one level this certainly makes sense: an in-office memo is not intended to inform the public, therefore the public interest in speech is probably less. This would seem to support the simple test suggested in the first paragraph of this section: was the speaker acting privately or as a government employee. Of course, if format *were* dispositive rather than just one factor, the *Connick* court would have treated the entire questionnaire as exempt from First Amendment protection as a wholly internal communication. That's not what it did—it interpreted "matter of public concern" as the *Pickering* court did, to refer to matters of interest to the community.

The District Attorney cases suggest a decline in free speech protection of government employees at the same time that the Court became more sympathetic to employer interests in other areas of the law. In *Rankin v. McPherson* (1987) (Marshall), however, the Court issued a surprising "pro-employee" speech ruling. McPherson, a clerk in the Constable's Office of Harris County, Texas, said something dreadful to a co-worker on the day President Reagan was shot. The statement was, "if they go for him again, I hope they get him." She was fired and challenged her dismissal on First Amendment grounds. A majority overturned the firing, emphasizing that the *Pickering* test applied because the life of the President is a matter of public concern. Topic, not format, was the key question in this pre-*Garcetti* case. The fact that the statement was in no way a serious contribution to public debate did not change this fact (it is likely that in context, her statement was an over-the-top rhetorical conclusion to a series of comments about specific Reagan Administration policies). The balancing test also favored the speech: McPherson's comments automatically had some weight because even imprudent or disrespectful speech has some value in the marketplace, and, more importantly, the Constable never explained how the statement had harmed the office atmosphere. The Court looked at numerous facts, and found ways to distinguish McPherson's offensive comment from threats or other speech that facilitates illegal conduct, two categories that would not be protected. **Why do we read and discuss this? Not so much to get a definitive statement as opposed to a rhetorical question: Why does, "kill the President" get First Amendment protection but "police officers are lying in search warrant applications" doesn't?**

In 2014, the Court issued another important decision favorable to government employee speakers. In *Lane v. Franks* (Sotomayor), the Court concluded that an Alabama Community College violated the First Amendment when it fired a person because he testified against a corrupt state legislator who had demanded a no-show job from a public job-training program managed by the college. The holding limited some of the implications of *Connick* and *Garcetti*. Lane's speech was courtroom testimony given under subpoena rather than an internal memo, as in those cases. If that is all that distinguishes the cases, the additional speech protection is fairly limited, and requires a whistleblower's speech to result in a successful judicial action, all before the *Pickering* balancing test becomes applicable. On this view, there is presumably no protection for words used within the government employment relationship (although *Rankin* involved speech in a conversation between employees while at work). Still, the language of *Lane* is sufficiently broad to encompass most speech that escapes the office in some manner. It refocuses the inquiry on "public concern" as tied to public interest, which it defines as speech related to "any matter of political, social, or other concern to the community . . . a subject of legitimate news interest." The Court's description of the necessary countervailing governmental interest in the balancing test reverts to *Pickering's* presumed protection of speech, unless the speech itself is harmful to office operations.

What's the Takeaway (not just a running subtotal waiting for the next case)? **The Court is protective of government employee free speech rights when it gets to the balancing test. It gets to that test when it concludes that the speech was on a subject of public concern, and may require that the speech be communicated in a public setting.** Therefore it is important for government employee speakers to get their speech into a public channel. This should make it likely that a court will use the balancing test and not dismiss the case in a perfunctory manner because it is merely an internal communication. **That leads to why we read and discuss these cases. Running throughout is an emphasis on the importance of a full public discourse of issues through open channels of communications and alternative channels when some are closed: *Robust Public Debate*.**

B. Public Property

The Supreme Court has developed an entirely different set of rules to govern speech on public property. (We put most of this discussion in chapter 3, but we re-emphasize a bit here.) Early cases interpreted the common law to give governments the same rights to exclude as private property owners, which sharply limited free speech claims. In the first half of the 20th century, however, the Court developed the principle that certain types of property are held in trust for the public, and speech rights are protected. The initial application of the trust principle was to streets and parks, and this designation has survived in what is called forum analysis. The forum approach determines the extent to which courts should defer to government efforts to limit speech on public property. If the speech takes place at a *public forum*, such as the streets or parks, government gets no deference, let alone any special or additional power to regulate speech based on its status as owner. On the other hand, if the speech takes place at other government property called a *non-public forum*, courts generally defer, thereby giving government substantially more power to regulate speech than it would have as a lawmaker, although still not as much as a private property owner.

As noted, the typical public forum is a street or park. **If a government agency tries to regulate speech *based on content* at a public forum, it must satisfy Strict Scrutiny; if it regulates time, place, or manner without regard to content, it is subject to the lesser, quasi-Intermediate Scrutiny standard.** Stated differently, government has no more or less authority to regulate speech at a public forum than it has to regulate speech on private property. Simply apply the tests from chapter 3. Thus, a content-based regulation of picketing on public streets must satisfy Strict Scrutiny, and a content-neutral time, place, or manner restriction of sound levels at a park concert must satisfy quasi-Intermediate Scrutiny.

Identifying a public forum is not always easy. While streets and parks may be the only "organic" public forums, governments add to the category when they designate other property as a public forum. For example, public universities often allow student or community groups to use their facilities for speeches, debates, or other expressive activities. When they do so, they may be making those facilities *designated* public forums. Publicly owned theaters also count as designated public forums in some settings, and the same would seem true of rooms in libraries or public schools that are designated for such use. The extent of government power to limit free speech rights by terminating or otherwise limiting the "forum" aspect of a generally or previously available facility remains controversial.

Other government property falls in the non-public forum category (wouldn't it make more sense to call it a *public non-forum*?). This is simply the First Amendment category for public property that has a primary function *other* than speech or assembly (so do streets and parks, but ignore this anomaly). Most government-owned property fits into the non-public forum category: office buildings, courthouses, post offices, military bases, publicly-owned utilities, internal communications systems, and the like. **Speech in a non-public forum is governed by a "reasonableness" standard.** Government may limit or even ban many varieties of speech, as long as it does not engage in viewpoint discrimination—for example, allowing the Young Capitalists Cartel to use a public meeting room, but prohibiting a similar use by the Young Socialists Commune. Governments that are trying to do their job carefully should not find it hard to satisfy this standard. But the test is not as deferential as the Rational Basis test. Most years one student or another sees "reasonableness" in his or her notes and translates that for the exam as the same as the Rational Basis test from basic Constitutional Law. It's not.

C. Public Education

Public education has its own set of First Amendment rules. Most controversies involve speech by students, who are persons in the care of the government while at school (*in loco parentis*), which is usually public property. This suggests logical connections to both government as employer and as property owner. The thrust of analysis, however, typically concerns the rights of minors. One can see the difference by comparing public education cases with cases dealing with school teachers, which are typical "government employee" cases (*Pickering* is an example).

Until the middle of the 20th century, no one gave a lot of thought to the constitutional rights of young persons. Then, in what is still the leading public education First Amendment case, the Supreme Court held that students have First Amendment rights while at school. *Tinker v. Des Moines Independent Community School District* (1969) (Fortas) overturned the suspension of junior high and high school students for wearing armbands to protest the Vietnam War. The majority opinion is long on rhetoric but short on specifics. The key phrase is that students do not "shed their constitutional rights to freedom of speech or expression at the schoolhouse gate." As such, *Tinker* goes into the Supreme Court's Great Hall of Ringing Phrases, for judges and lawyers to trot out in litigation. What *Tinker* held was less helpful, but it still gives us a somewhat vague **Takeaway: Schools restricting speech by students violate the First Amendment unless they show that the speech is likely to obstruct classes or other school activities.** Since the teenagers in the case were involved in a sincere and non-disruptive protest, it would be hard to find any justification to ban their actions. On the other hand, free speech does not allow students to breach classroom etiquette. So, for example, standing up and interrupting classmates to give an impassioned defense of the First Amendment in the middle of class is not protected speech, even in a Constitutional Law class.

Most cases making their way to the Supreme Court since *Tinker* have involved students who are less serious and respectful in their speech and justices who are more willing to defer to sometimes unarticulated justifications for disciplining student expression. For example, in a case that had "less serious" speech, plus some disruption, the Court upheld the suspension of a student who gave a speech full of juvenile sexual innuendo at a school assembly. The Court concluded that the speech was inconsistent with the school's educational mission, which included teaching social and moral values, and made no contribution to legitimate debate, unlike the political protest in *Tinker*. In short, what passes for entertainment on the playground may still be disciplined at official school events.

A case that intrigues and entertains law students is *Morse v. Frederick* (2007) (Roberts), which involved the display of a banner proclaiming "BONG HiTS 4 JESUS." Students were released from class to watch the Olympic torch as it passed the school. Frederick unfurled the banner at the critical time—that is, just in time to catch the attention of television cameras covering the torch relay. The principal interpreted the message as promoting drug use, confiscated the banner, and suspended the student holding the banner. The Supreme Court's majority was very deferential to the principal's determinations, concluding that punishing advocacy of drug use is within school authority. (Of course, the real meaning of "bong hits for Jesus" remains unknown, and is the subject of debate in cyberspace.)

Why do we read and discuss these cases? Most commentators make two overriding points, which you can use to navigate your way through a school speech case. **The first is the basic principle from** *Tinker*: **students retain First Amendment rights while in school, and therefore are presumptively allowed to express themselves,**

at least where the academic justification to limit speech is not self-evident. **The second point is that schools may prevent or punish speech that disrupts the educational mission.** Principals and other school disciplinarians have learned over the years that courts are likely to defer to their judgment when they have reasonable explanations for why the speech disrupts the educational environment. (Note the similar concerns and analysis when looking at Fourth Amendment rights and searches (including drug testing) of students in the school setting.)

D. Spending

Much government policymaking is implemented through appropriations—spending money. Rather than regulating conduct to achieve preferred results, government funds activities it supports, both through direct grants and by using appropriations to promote those activities. In theory, spending could violate the First Amendment in two ways. First, government could spend to reward persons or groups based on what the persons or groups *say*. This would discourage the public from engaging in speech that differs from government policies. Second, government could impose conditions on accepting government financial support. That is, it could award funds on condition that the recipient says what the government wants it to say (or refrains from saying what the government does not want it to say).

One preliminary question is whether the First Amendment even applies to such passive speech restrictions. **When government considers private speech in deciding how to spend, it neither prevents nor punishes speech, as it does when it imposes criminal or civil liability or deprives a speaker of a valuable interest, such as a job.** This fact would support nearly automatic First Amendment approval of a government power to consider speech in making spending decisions. Some justices take this view, at least some of the time. Still, presumably the "coercion" analysis of federal spending powers applies here. For example, if the government were to offer a very substantial sum to a couple of law professors to withdraw their First Amendment book, it might constitute an offer they couldn't refuse, in the *Godfather* sense (if you don't get the reference, just call us). If so, spending can be a regulation in substance.

Many of the controversies about the impact of government spending on First Amendment interests end up mooted because a reviewing court concludes that the speech at issue was that of the government rather than of a private person. For example, *Rust v. Sullivan* (1991) (Rehnquist) involved speech restrictions about abortion services that were required by the federal law that funded family-planning services. In a close decision, the Supreme Court held that the funding limitation was the government's way of implementing its own policy preference against spending in support of abortions. The doctors in effect became federal agents, and following the statutory script was part of their job, not an interference with their own freedom of speech. Presumably, they would remain free to speak about family planning issues, as shown in the government employment section. In a very different setting, the Court used the same reasoning to uphold Texas's right to disapprove a specialty license plate celebrating confederate veterans. A license plate motto, like a state promotional billboard or policy statement, is a vehicle for communicating the *government's views*, and would not normally affect individual free speech.

Cases are more difficult where the government funding weighs either in favor of or against private expression. In one notable case, *National Endowment for the Arts v. Finley* (1998) (O'Connor), a provocative performance artist challenged the National Endowment for the Arts' denial of her application for a federal grant. The enabling statute provided that grants were to be judged by artistic merit, "taking into consideration general standards of decency and respect for the diverse beliefs and values of the American public." The Court upheld the statutory admonition to consider these factors, despite the fact that they seemed to invite "soft" censorship by favoring non-controversial applications. The Court emphasized that the case did not involve viewpoint discrimination, which would have raised serious First Amendment concerns. That implies that a decision choosing one of two essentially equally worthy applications specifically because of the winner's adherence to the government's viewpoint would violate this principle. For example, if a government agency sponsored a law school moot court competition in which the issue was abortion rights, and then awarded victory to a team because it took the position most like that of the sponsoring government rather to the team with the best advocates, it would probably violate the First Amendment.

As noted above, conditions present another setting in which government can try to influence private speech through the spending power. One case in which a government condition was upheld is *Regan v. Taxation with Representation* (1997) (Rehnquist), which challenged a statutory ban on lobbying by tax-exempt organizations. Nothing in the restriction prevented organizations from lobbying (presumably a constitutional right under the Petition clause of the First Amendment); the condition was that organizations accepting tax-exempt status do so on condition that they not lobby Congress. The Court concluded that Congress simply chose not to provide financial support for lobbying through the tax code, which was within its discretion. On the other hand, had Congress decided to allow tax exemptions for lobbying *on certain issues*, such as abortion or corporate tax benefits, the likely conclusion would be that by picking sides on the basis of viewpoint, Congress's spending crossed the line to "abridge" the speech of those who do not share that viewpoint.

Legal Services Corp. v. Velazquez (2001) (Kennedy) presented another setting and a different outcome. Federal grants to legal services organizations prohibited recipients from making certain arguments in representing clients, primarily challenging welfare laws. The condition in effect meant that attorneys funded by the Legal Services Corporation were limited in the services they could provide their clients. A close decision struck down the condition, concluding that by limiting the arguments an attorney may make, the condition improperly interfered with the attorney's professional responsibility to represent his or her clients. This distinguishes cases in which government imposes a limitation on *private* speech—disallowed in *Velazquez*—from those in which government chooses the terms and conditions of speech on *behalf of government*—allowed in *Rust*. Finally, government may not impose conditions on how funds from other sources may be used. That would be considered a backdoor attempt to regulate private speech.

What's the Takeaway? It depends. First Amendment doctrine on spending is intricate and requires close attention to what may seem like slight technical distinctions in statutory or regulatory language. Spending therefore joins government employment (largely a balancing test), government property (a functional approach that channels into the more general constitutional tests of Strict and Intermediate Scrutiny), and public education (a very general balancing test) to make a scattered legal framework for the law regulating government when it acts in special roles.

THINGS TO KNOW

- Public employees who speak in a private capacity on matters of public concern receive First Amendment protections.

- That protection is determined through a balancing test that weighs the value of the speech against the adverse effect on operations of the employing agency.

- Forum analysis: Public forums (standard First Amendment rules); Non-public forums (general reasonableness).

- Students have First Amendment rights at school, but schools may prohibit speech that is disruptive or that promotes illegal conduct.

- The intersection of spending and the First Amendment is unusually complex. Focus on issues such as, is this government speech?, is the government rewarding or disadvantaging speakers because of their viewpoint?, is there a reasonable limitation on use of public funds?

THINGS TO THINK ABOUT

- The First Amendment tends to give government more authority in special roles than it has as lawmaker, but less than a private person. Is this intermediate position fully justified?

- The Court has chosen a variety of different methods to implement this intermediate position. Would a simpler, more unified approach work, or at least work better.

CHAPTER 5

Political Speech and Association

This chapter explores questions of political speech and association, and that will raise competing theories of the meaning of the First Amendment. In terms of political activity, we see First Amendment issues in the form of actual speech, as well as in terms of the regulations of political campaigns, fundraising and spending.

A. Political Speech

Speech is at the core of our democratic process, an essential part of "a profound national commitment to the principle that debate on public issues should be uninhibited, robust, and wide-open." The best ideas must be put out there, and debated, and the people can choose what ideas they find persuasive. In that regard, by allowing each of us our own freedom to speak individually, and all of us to shop in the marketplace of ideas, we ultimately decide how we want to govern.

In that sense, the First Amendment can be seen as the guarantor of a participatory democracy, where the people are essential to the project of governance. This conception of speech echoes The Declaration of Independence: governments derive "their just powers from the consent of the governed." Likewise Justice Brandeis articulated this core understanding of the First Amendment in his concurring opinion in *Whitney v. California*: "those who won our independence believed that public discussion is a political duty; and that this should be a fundamental principle of the American government."

Because the First Amendment fosters the process of open discussion, that empowers the people to speak freely and to safely vent ideas, frustrations, and anger. In doing so without government interference, the broader debate is enriched, and ideas are tested. In cases like *Cohen v. California*, we see the First Amendment allowing and protecting dissident speech, so as to allow the people to debate and decide the pressing issues of our society. (See Chapter 2.) The remedy for alienation and discontent is not less, but more free expression of ideas; in this way, the First Amendment acts as a safety valve for our system. Unrestrained expression not only allows ideas to be put out there, but for the proponents to let their own emotion show, much like a steam valve allows for the escape of pressure so as to prevent a buildup that causes an explosion.

Some argue that all political speech should be unfettered, as the lifeblood of our democracy. But not everybody has an equal ability to speak on public issues, spend in campaigns, and/or contribute to candidates. In particular, those who have money have a greater ability to present their views (through spending) than those who lack resources. You might reply, *So what?* One approach, famously espoused by Alexander Meiklejohn, puts free speech at the heart of democracy: he argued that when the less wealthy are silenced because the more wealthy are loud, we may quiet the loud/rich ones, so as to ensure that quiet/poor are heard. We balance speech so that all may be heard in our democracy. The counterargument is that by following Meiklejohn's approach, you silence the speech rights of the individual seeking to speak. The key question then becomes whether the government may restrict speech (or financial expenditures) of some participants in the marketplace of ideas in order to lessen the impact of the differences in the amount of money available to one side or the other and thus "improve" overall quality of public debate? Myriad competing values play out in the context of speech rights in the political process.

With that background, we explore several specific areas of interest, starting with **money and politics**, the most prominent topic of discussion. The pivotal 1976 *per curiam* decision in *Buckley v. Valeo* defined the landscape in this field. The case arose in the immediate aftermath of Pres. Nixon's resignation in the wake of the Watergate scandal. Congress passed sweeping reforms to federal election law, including limits on campaign contributions and expenditures. In ruling on a challenge to these laws, the Court's key analytical move was to equate money and speech—the Court declared spending on political matters to be protected First Amendment expressive activity. The question that follows is, if money is speech, why can Congress regulate at all? Regulating fundamental rights requires a compelling governmental interest, after all. The Court struck down limits on campaign spending, rejecting the idea that limiting the skyrocketing costs of campaigns would justify (constitutionally speaking) capping campaign expenditures. The Court held: "It is argued . . . that the ancillary governmental interest in equalizing the relative ability of individuals and groups to influence the outcome of elections serves to justify the limitations. . . . But the concept that government may restrict the speech of some elements of our society in order to enhance the relative voice of others is wholly foreign to the First Amendment." While the Justices rejected *spending* limits, they upheld *contribution* limits. The Court held that capping contributions is permissible because it is only a marginal restriction on a lesser speech interest. Most importantly, the government restriction was justified by an interest in preventing corruption or the appearance thereof. In effect, the holding was justified because of concerns about corruption in the process, in the context of Watergate.

What's the Takeaway? Broadly, money is equated with speech; specifically, political spending in campaigns cannot be restricted by the government. Contributions to candidates can be limited only in order to meet the compelling government interest in preventing actual *quid pro quo* corruption, or the appearance thereof.

Why do we read and discuss *Buckley*? First and foremost, it is the foundational case in the area of money, speech and politics. Forty years later, it is still the touchstone. But while *Buckley* has controlled the Court's analysis, there has been increasing discontent (for a wide variety of reasons) on the Court about the decision. Justice Thomas has been *Buckley's* most vocal critic in recent years, arguing that contribution limits improperly suppress speech and should be subject to strict scrutiny, which they cannot survive. As he has written: "I continue to believe that [*Buckley*] should be overruled. 'Political speech is the primary object of First Amendment protection,' and it is the lifeblood of a self-governing people." Justice Kennedy has been dissatisfied with *Buckley's* contribution vs. expenditure distinction, arguing that "[t]he compromise the Court invented in *Buckley* set the stage for a new kind of speech to enter the political system. It is covert speech. The Court has forced a substantial amount of speech underground, as contributors and candidates devise ever more elaborate methods of avoiding contribution limits." When he was on the Court, Justice Stevens notably objected from another perspective, finding fault with the entire *Buckley* analysis, because "Money is property; it is not speech." In a related vein, Justice Breyer has challenged the money-as-speech premise, suggesting a need to reconsider *Buckley*.

"(A) decision to contribute money to a campaign is a matter of First Amendment concern—not because money is speech (it is not); but because it *enables* speech." With such divergent opinions, there is no consensus as to whether *Buckley* should be overruled, and if so, what new standard should emerge. And in considering these different perspectives, we also consider the central meaning of the First Amendment itself. In the end *Buckley* still is the controlling paradigm—so we have to know what it says and what it means.

Over the intervening years, the Court reviewed a wide range of campaign finance reform measures, struggling to enforce the rule of *Buckley* in a consistent manner, in both facial and as-applied challenges. Most notably, in *McConnell v. FEC* (2003) the Court largely upheld the Bipartisan Campaign Reform Act of 2002 ("BCRA"). In major part BCRA attempted to control "soft money" (funds that were used in ways designed to evade the "hard money" contribution limits on candidates and political parties) and "issue advocacy" (advertisements that were designed to influence an election result but spoke more about an issue than an individual candidate). One notable feature was a limit on "electioneering communications", *i.e.*, independent expenditures that expressly advocate for or against a candidate. The statute prohibited "any broadcast . . . that 'refers to a clearly identified candidate for Federal office' and made within 30 days of a primary or 60 days of a general election." Showing some deference to the federal rules and acknowledging a concern for the corrupting effects of circumventing those limits, a divided Court upheld almost all of BCRA (on its face); still, this decision was a facial challenge, and a shaky future lay ahead.

The unsettled landscape changed dramatically in 2010 in *Citizens United v. FEC* (Kennedy), as the Court held that corporations and unions enjoy First Amendment protection, just like individuals, in the context of political spending. As a result, corporations and unions can contribute and spend large sums of money in order to sway elections and impact the political process. In the 2008 presidential campaign cycle Citizens United (a nonprofit corporation) released a film entitled: *Hillary: The Movie*, a 90-minute mostly negative and critical documentary about then-Senator Clinton while she was a candidate for the presidency. The film was clearly intended to inform the viewer about Citizens United's opinion of Clinton's fitness to be President. The movie was released on DVD and in theaters, as well as being available through Video-on-Demand; Citizens United also produced promotional advertisements. Citizens United's plan ran afoul of BCRA, which prohibited corporations and unions from using general funds to make direct contributions to candidates or to make electioneering communications. Citizens United sought relief against the Federal Election Commission, arguing in large part that BCRA was unconstitutional as applied. The Court agreed and dramatically changed the landscape of campaign finance and First Amendment protection of money in politics; at least as dramatically as the *Buckley* decision.

What's the Takeaway? First, the Court struck down the specific provision of BCRA, not just as-applied, but on its face as well. Next, the heart of the majority's argument is as follows: (1) money and political spending can be equated with protected speech; (2) corporations can be considered as natural persons with First Amendment speech rights; and therefore (3) BCRA's restriction on corporate spending improperly violates the First Amendment. Justice Kennedy wrote: "[i]f the First Amendment has any force, it prohibits Congress from fining or jailing citizens, or associations of citizens, for simply engaging in political speech."

Why do we read this case? The *Citizens United* opinion may be described as a triumph of the First Amendment over government attempts to regulate core protected political speech. As Justice

Kennedy framed the majority opinion, the Court's concern was our nation's commitment to vigorous unrestrained debate on all matters pertaining to our politics and government. There can be no doubt that the Constitution places a premium on free expression and the First Amendment. While the Court appropriately celebrated the First Amendment, it did not adequately address the importance of equality concerns in our democracy. There is a tension here: one constitutional value gets promoted over another. In this context, free speech interests effectively trump equality interests. These are the ongoing debates in this field.

The next year in *Arizona Free Enterprise Club v. Bennett* (Roberts), the Supreme Court threw out a provision of Arizona's public campaign financing system. Arizona enacted a campaign finance law that provided matching funds to candidates who accepted public financing. The law, passed in 1998, gave an initial sum to candidates for state office who accept public financing and then gave additional matching funds based on the amounts spent by privately financed opponents and by independent groups. Those who wanted to spend more than the state gave, could do so. But when those better-funded candidates spent larger sums, that triggered an additional payment to the state-funded candidates, in order to try to equalize overall spending from private dollars. In 2008, some candidates and a political action committee, the Arizona Free Enterprise Club, filed suit arguing that to avoid triggering matching funds for their opponents, they had to limit their spending and, in essence, their freedom of speech. They claimed the law that gave campaign funds to candidates actually limited the speech rights of the wealthy self-funding candidates.

The Court broadly held that the triggered matching fund provisions of Arizona's public financing system substantially burdened First Amendment rights of privately financed candidates for public office, as well as independent expenditure groups, without a sufficiently compelling government interest. The law didn't survive Strict Scrutiny. The Court also held that public financing is an acceptable vehicle to combat corruption or the appearance of corruption so long as it is "pursued in a manner consistent with the First Amendment," but Arizona's program went "too far". As a result the Court threw out the trigger fund provisions in Arizona and in other public campaign financing programs.

Justice Kagan argued in dissent that this marks a "world gone topsy-turvy", and that "[t]his suit, in fact, may merit less attention than any challenge to a speech subsidy ever seen in this Court. . . . Arizona, remember, offers to support any person running for state office. Petitioners here *refused* that assistance. So they are making a novel argument: that Arizona violated their First Amendment rights by disbursing funds to *other* speakers even though they could have received (but chose to spurn) the same financial assistance." Speaking to the theory we have been considering, Justice Kagan added, "The First Amendment's core purpose is to foster a healthy, vibrant political system full of robust discussion and debate. . . . Nothing in Arizona's anti-corruption statute violates this constitutional protection. To the contrary, the Act promotes the values underlying both the First Amendment and our entire Constitution by enhancing the 'opportunity for free political discussion to the end that government may be responsive to the will of the people.' "

What's the Takeaway? The Court has not only held that limiting spending violates a candidate's free speech rights, but also government spending to *equalize* the amount of money spent by candidates violates First Amendment rights of the self-financed candidate. Speech rights trump equality concerns. This not only echoes *Buckley*, but also *R.A.V.* (see Chapter 2).

The most recent case in this field is 2014's *McCutcheon v. FEC* (Roberts), in which the Court struck down aggregate contribution limits—the amount one contributor can give in federal elections to all candidates, political parties, and PACs, combined. This marks the first time the Supreme Court has declared a federal contribution limit unconstitutional. In striking down these limits, the Court in effect held that using political campaign contributions to gain access and influence is a key democratic right. Practically speaking, the decision allows candidates and parties to collect substantially larger sums from individual donors. **What's the Takeaway? Individuals are free to contribute to as many candidates, political parties and PACs as they want. Further, with the Court striking down this federal contribution limit, many wonder whether other contribution limits may soon fall.**

Why do we read and discuss *McCutcheon* (and *Bennett*)? In these last two cases, the Court has solidified a very significant shift toward deregulating campaign spending, under a First Amendment analysis. The Court is saying that free spending of money trumps the idea that we can equalize voices in politics, so as to create a more even debate. The majority finds that unlimited political spending is (constitutionally-speaking) more important than trying to create a level playing field for political discourse. In some ways, this is the ultimate statement that money equals speech, perhaps most fitting in our country that is defined by two major institutions: capitalism and democracy.

B. Right of Association

The Court has protected the right of association in a handful of cases, in which the Justices see the freedom to associate as central to our democratic processes. In these cases, the Court also seems wary of governmental intent, in similar ways to what we saw in our analysis of time, place, and manner restrictions (see Chapter 3).

The seminal cases came in the context of the Civil Rights movement, in *NAACP v. Alabama* (1958) (Harlan) and *NAACP v.*

Button (1963) (Brennan). In the first case, the Alabama Attorney General sought to enjoin the NAACP—a national association—from conducting business within the State. The Attorney General moved for the production of some of the NAACP's records and papers, including a list of the names and addresses of all of its Alabama members. The NAACP had evidence that in the past, revealing their members' identities "has exposed these members to economic reprisal, loss of employment, threat of physical coercion, and other manifestations of public hostility." Therefore, disclosure of the list would adversely affect the Association's ability to advance its beliefs; members would withdraw and others would be discouraged from joining in fear of the negative consequences of exposure. The specific question before the Court was whether Alabama could compel the discovery. In his opinion for the Court, Justice Harlan held that compelled disclosure of the membership list excessively burdened the members' right to engage in lawful association in support of their common beliefs, without a sufficient state interest to justify it. "Whether there was 'justification' in this instance turns solely on the substantiality of Alabama's interest in obtaining the membership lists." The State did not have a sufficient interest to interfere with the members' right to freely associate in order to privately advocate for and foster their common beliefs.

A few years later, Justice Brennan wrote for the Court in *NAACP v. Button*. There, the State of Virginia sought to restrict certain of the NAACP's litigation activities on behalf of its members and others. That litigation was designed to assist potential parties in asserting specific constitutional rights and to help achieve constitutional equality more broadly. These litigation activities were protected by the First Amendment. The Court held that the Virginia regulation infringed on the NAACP's right to associate for the purpose of providing legal assistance to people whose legal rights have been violated. The regulation unduly burdened these protected freedoms without a compelling state interest to justify it;

the State's alleged interest to ensure high professional standards did not justify the prohibition of the NAACP.

What's the Takeaway? First Amendment associational rights are protected from state interference without sufficient justification. Heightened scrutiny is required.

Why do we read these cases? In *Button* Justice Douglas concurred to offer an even more pointed analysis than the majority that helps our understanding. He wrote "This Virginia Act is not applied across the board to all groups that use this method of obtaining and managing litigation, but instead reflects a legislative purpose to penalize the N. A. A. C. P. because it promotes desegregation of the races." He traced a line from *Brown v. Board of Education* through to this statute (and four others) in Virginia, as well as five other States' similar actions, all part of "massive resistance" against the Court's prior decisions. He concluded that Virginia (and these other Southern states) sought only to "evade our prior decisions" in *Brown* and elsewhere, and that they were targeted to stifling the activities of the NAACP. The right of association thus was tied to a broader social movement, and that helps us see the importance of association rights in terms of the people's ability to engage in self-governance. The states acted with a transparent intent to squelch this associational activity to bring about change; this *intent* was harmful, perhaps fatal, to the government's attempt to regulate.

Moving forward in time, three more cases shed additional light. In *Roberts v. United States Jaycees* (1984), Justice Brennan again wrote for the Court to analyze associational rights. The U.S. Jaycees was an organization founded for the purpose of fostering the growth of young men, limiting regular membership to men between 18 and 35 years old, while older men and women could only be associate members, without voting and other rights. After the Minneapolis and St. Paul chapters began allowing women to become regular members in violation of the national bylaws, the national organization considered revoking its charter. Members of both chapters filed discrimination complaints with the Minnesota Department of Human Rights. The local chapter members argued that the Minnesota Human Rights Act prohibited unfair discrimination in places of public accommodation and would require the Jaycees to accept women as regular members. The national Jaycees argued that requiring it to admit women as regular members violated its members' associational rights.

The constitutional question became whether Minnesota could require the Jaycees to admit women as regular members without violating the First (and Fourteenth) Amendment rights of the organization's members. Using Strict Scrutiny analysis, the Court held that applying the Minnesota antidiscrimination law to the Jaycees was the least restrictive means for achieving a compelling state interest. The Jaycees was a large and basically unselective group (age and sex were the only criteria used to judge applicants), which did not help a claim of a violation of the group's freedom of expressive association. While requiring the Jaycees to admit women as full voting members may have interfered with the internal affairs of the association, any "[i]nfringements on that right may be justified by regulations adopted to serve compelling state interests, unrelated to the suppression of ideas, that cannot be achieved through means significantly less restrictive of associational freedoms." On the other hand, the Court held that Minnesota had a compelling interest in combating gender discrimination that justified infringing on the male members' freedom of association.

What's the Takeaway? Strict Scrutiny applies when making this First Amendment analysis. The Court held that the state's compelling interest in eradicating discrimination against women justified the impact that application of the act may have on some men's associational freedoms. There was a sufficient state interest to justify regulating the associational rights that the U.S. Jaycees sought to protect. The First Amendment right to association is not absolute.

Why do we read this? Importantly, Justice Brennan's opinion noted that the regulation was not related to suppressing any specific ideas or perspectives. The idea of viewpoint-neutrality comes into play in yet another context.

About ten years later in *Hurley v. Irish-American Gay, Lesbian and Bisexual Group of Boston* (1995) (Souter), the Court rejected the City of Boston's attempt to require the organizers to include GLIB—a group self-identified as gays, lesbians and bisexuals—in the St. Patrick's Day parade. GLIB applied to march in the parade as a unit, in order to express their Irish heritage pride as openly gay, lesbian, and bisexual individuals. GLIB was formed for the purpose of expressing its members' sexual identities and Irish heritage in the existing parade. The parade organizers denied the request; GLIB alleged violations of the Constitution and of the state public accommodations law. The question thus was whether the State would violate the First Amendment by mandating that a group (GLIB) march in the parade and express a message the organizers did not wish to convey.

This carried First Amendment implications because parades are a form of expression and are protected conduct under the First Amendment. As a matter of free association, the Court held that private citizens who organize a parade cannot be forced to include a group who express a message the organizers do not want to express. "The protected expression that inheres in a parade is not limited to its banners and songs, however, for the Constitution looks beyond written or spoken words as mediums of expression." The Court upheld the exclusion of GLIB. The individual GLIB members could have still marched with any group approved by the Council, or could have obtained a permit to organize their own parade.

"Although each parade unit generally identifies itself, each is understood to contribute something to a common theme, and accordingly there is no customary practice whereby private sponsors disavow 'any identity of viewpoint' between themselves and the selected participants." The Court held that Massachusetts did not have a sufficient interest to apply the public accommodations law to the parade because the law "is not free to interfere with speech for no better reason than promoting an approved message or discouraging a disfavored one, however enlightened either purpose may strike the government." Thus the case was about speech and expressive activities, but still fit within the tradition of free association, protecting the parade organizers' ability to define themselves as they saw fit, without state interference.

Finally, in 2000 the Court ruled in *Boy Scouts of America v. Dale* (Rehnquist) that the Boy Scouts had an associational right to exclude homosexuals from certain leadership positions. Dale, an adult Boy Scout leader, argued that the Boy Scouts had violated New Jersey's public accommodations law by revoking his membership because of his sexual orientation. The Boy Scouts countered by saying that application of the statute in that way would violate the First Amendment. Given the Scouts' mission to instill values in youth by adult leaders' expressions and examples, they argued that Dale's presence would have forced a message that the group accepted homosexual conduct. This, they claimed, violated the First Amendment rights of expression and association.

The Court held that requiring the Boy Scouts to retain Dale as a member was a severe intrusion on the Boy Scouts' right to freedom of expressive association that was not justified by New Jersey's interest in its public accommodations law. "The forced inclusion of an unwanted person in a group infringes the group's freedom of expressive association if the presence of that person affects in a significant way the group's ability to advocate public or private viewpoints." Chief Justice Rehnquist wrote that keeping Dale in his leadership role would significantly burden the Boy Scouts because his message was inconsistent with the values the Boy Scouts seek to instill in their members, specifically its belief that homosexual conduct is not "morally straight". The Court re-stated a Strict Scrutiny standard, opining that the freedom of expressive association could still be lawfully limited "by regulations adopted to serve compelling state interests, unrelated to the suppression of ideas, that cannot be achieved through means significantly less restrictive of associational freedoms." But here, New Jersey's interests were held not to justify this intrusion: "public or judicial disapproval of a tenet of an organization's expression does not justify the State's effort to compel the organization to accept members where such acceptance would derogate from the organization's expressive message." Dissenting, Justices Stevens and Souter argued that the New Jersey public accommodations law did not impose a substantial burden on the Boy Scouts because it did not interfere with their ability to express shared goals or force the Boy Scouts to endorse a view they did not believe in, especially because the Boy Scouts had never previously conveyed an opinion on sexual orientation: "no group can claim a right of expressive association without identifying a clear position to be advocated over time in an unequivocal way."

What's the Takeaway? The majority in *Dale* re-stated a Strict Scrutiny standard for First Amendment expressive association, holding that the government may act in this field only "by regulations adopted to serve compelling state interests, unrelated to the suppression of ideas, that cannot be achieved through means significantly less restrictive of associational freedoms."

Why do we read these cases? We see a similar debate from the earlier NAACP and *Roberts* cases, but with some twists. Both then and now, the government sought to regulate private organizations, and the Court struck down the state regulation. Then, the Court upheld the associational rights of the NAACP, in what was seen as a progressive step forward in protecting the work of the civil rights movement. In *Dale* and *Hurley*, the Court again rejected the state's regulation, but it was not seen as a progressive move, and it was seen as contrary to the advancing the civil rights of the individuals who claimed discrimination. Note also that in 2015, the Boston parade organizers allowed for the first gay groups to march in the parade. That same year, the national leadership of the Boy Scouts of America lifted the ban on openly gay adult Scout leaders.

THINGS TO KNOW

- Money is constitutional speech, or at least a necessary means to making political speech effective.

- The Supreme Court has applied Strict Scrutiny to prevent most federal and state attempts to limit political spending by candidates, individuals, corporations, and unions.

- Individuals and groups have a First Amendment right of expressive association that requires government regulations that restrict associational freedoms to satisfy Strict Scrutiny.

THINGS TO THINK ABOUT

- What better serves the underlying purposes of the First Amendment? Allowing all support of political speech, thereby enabling the wealthiest to drown out most of the rest of us, or equalizing political speech by limiting expenditures on political issues, which necessarily prevents some political speech?

- Is there a danger that creating a broad freedom of association right will "constitutionalize" private discrimination?

CHAPTER 6

The Internet and New Media

The development of the internet and other new electronic means of expression and communication logically requires original and creative application of First Amendment doctrine. The internet allows us to communicate faster, easier, and with a much wider distribution. It took months (and lots of paper and physical effort) for Daniel Ellsberg to photocopy and mail copies of the Pentagon Papers (call us, ask your parents, or just read through to Chapter 7) to just a handful of newspapers in 1969. But that can now be accomplished in the brief flurry of mouse clicks, as when Edward Snowden sent thousands of confidential United States documents to WikiLeaks, which then made them available to everyone everywhere. Those whose personnel or credit files have been breached by hackers know that internet recordkeeping and information technology is a very mixed blessing. On balance, the fact that the internet expands opportunities for people to spread pernicious or private information would seem to call for some doctrinal response.

While we haven't yet talked about any case law in this Chapter, we already have a key **Takeaway: in this area (is it even a field?), there has been little new doctrine, just old doctrine applied in new settings.** On reflection, this should not really be a major surprise. The telephone gave immediacy to the previously super-slow communication of handwritten letters, and the efficiencies of modern printing technology made books and newspapers inexpensive, making it possible and ultimately necessary for almost everyone to learn how to read. The internet and other new technologies have similarly changed the game, but not necessarily the *rules* of the game. The significant changes are most obvious in social effects that complicate freedom of speech in real life. Here are five examples:

1) It is easy to set up a website and publish information to the rest of the world. Such information can be wonderful or worse than disgusting.

2) As a result, this universal marketplace of ideas allows a lot of extremists to find like-minded individuals and to network with them.

3) Young people, always the savviest users of new technology, are exposed to a great deal of material for which they are unlikely to be prepared.

4) Once the Enter key is pressed, an email or post is probably accessible for ever (if not longer).

5) Highly skilled hackers are able to access and then distribute on the internet much information that always was private in the past.

You can probably come up with another five examples without working very hard at it.

These dislocations of new electronic technology have not had a lot of effect on First Amendment law. Instead, they have provided new and vexing settings for old First Amendment law. This chapter addresses four areas where this has taken place: 1) sexually explicit material, 2) threats, or statements perceived to be threatening, 3) defamatory content, and 4) violent content.

A. Sexually Explicit Material

Perhaps the most likely target for revised First Amendment analysis is sexually explicit content. The internet is the world's largest adult video store; rather, it is all of them at once. It is not hard to access pornography on the internet (just go see the Broadway musical *Avenue Q*, if you want puppets to sing an explanation)—generally all a person has to do in order to enter a pornographic website is affirm that he or she is at least 18. Obscenity and child pornography may be banned from internet sites because they are excluded from First Amendment protection generally and may be barred everywhere (see chapter 2). But this does not prevent young persons from viewing highly objectionable material just a touch "cleaner" than obscene.

Congress has passed some laws, most of which have been ineffective at limiting pornographic internet sites. In the Communications Decency Act of 1996, Congress criminalized making indecent or patently offensive material available to persons under 18. In *Reno v. ACLU* (1997) (Stevens), the Supreme Court found the law vague and overbroad, and saw no justification for applying a broader definition of obscenity than applies to any other medium. The Court expressly refused to follow the broadcasting regulation model, which is deferential to government power to regulate content, including offensive language readily accessible to young people. The majority opinion is notable for the assertion that the internet is *not* as invasive as television, a claim that no one would make today. This could provide a basis for rethinking the problem.

Congress responded with a new law, the Child Online Protection Act. The new law regulated sexually explicit web sites by requiring persons providing sexual content to prevent access by minors through at least one of several techniques, such as requiring credit cards in order to verify age. In *Ashcroft v. ACLU* (2004) (Kennedy), the Supreme Court held that the First Amendment invalidated the law because there were less restrictive ways to achieve the purpose of preventing young people from accessing adult web sites. For example, filtering software could be used by adults to prevent their children from accessing inappropriate material. In short, because the statute imposed restrictions at the website level, it burdened all persons, including adults who have a right to access the material, while filters, which are used at the receiving end at the direction and discretion of the computer's owner, empower responsible adults. This analysis is pretty much out of date, as minors are likely to control their own computers today. Nonetheless, the attempts to prevent *websites* from allowing young people to access sexually explicit material have not succeeded. **Free adult websites are generally accessible to all who claim to be 18. Commercial adult websites generally require credit card payment, the sort of age-verification system the Supreme Court held could not be required by statute in *Ashcroft*.** Presumably this makes it harder for young people to access pornography, but not impossible, as most such websites have free sections packed with pornography to encourage paid subscriptions.

Not all congressional actions in this area have failed. In *United States v. American Library Ass'n* (2003) (Rehnquist), the Court upheld the Children's Internet Protection Act. The law requires libraries and schools that accept federal technology funding to install filters to block access to pornographic websites on their computers used by minors. Rather than basing its decision on anything special about the internet, the plurality focused on the substantial discretion Congress has in using its *spending power* (haven't thought much about that since Con Law, have you?). **What's the Takeaway? Requiring that libraries use filters is a reasonable means of ensuring that the technology purchased with federal funds allows children to access only the non-pornographic materials that Congress intended them to be able to access.** As noted, even that conclusion represented only a plurality view, as two concurring justices emphasized that libraries could not use filters to prevent adult patrons from viewing blocked images or text. **Why do we read and discuss this? To emphasize that old doctrine applies to new technology, and new technology enjoys broad First Amendment protection.** Thus, while the government has not found a theory under which it can prevent or even limit access to pornographic materials on a person's *own* computer, at least it doesn't have to spend public funds to help the person do so on a *public* computer and internet connection.

B. Threats

Emails, texts, website comment features, and various smartphone applications all make it very easy to receive, react, and reply without thinking about it beforehand, which is convenient but dangerous. In the old days (*i.e.*, before the 1990s), people had to write angry memos on paper and put them in the U.S. mail. This took time. Sometimes they changed their minds and were able to retrieve their angry memo before it reached the addressee. In fact, some people learned to place their angry memos in a desk drawer immediately after writing, so that they could consider whether or not to send it for a day or two. Quite a few people wish our email systems would detect an angry reply and slip it into the *Drafts* folder for a cooling off period before it is sent. Thus, one social effect of immediate electronic communication is that lots of angry, sometimes threatening, communications are sent before the writer thinks it over.

Threats over electronic media have resulted in criminal and civil liability. Examples include charges of making email threats against politicians (*State v. Wooden*, Missouri), Facebook threats (*In re P.T.*, Ohio), and frightening postings on a website (*Raub v. Campbell*, E.D. Va.). These cases have two things in common: they recognize the increased likelihood of rude (or worse) discourse via electronic media, and they are decided on the basis of legal principles developed almost entirely in cases dealing with old technology, such as mail, telephones, and physical stalking. The Supreme Court has not weighed in here. It was expected to do so in 2015 when it considered *Elonis v. United States* (Roberts). This was a federal prosecution for making threats in interstate commerce, a much broader application than electronic communications, but probably the federal crime most applicable to threatening speech on the internet. Elonis posted something purporting to be rap lyrics on a pseudonymous Facebook page that seemed to threaten his wife (who left him), co-workers (who should have left him), and law enforcement officers (who apparently wouldn't leave him alone). In the end, the Court declined to focus on the nature of threats by social media and instead interpreted the statute's *mens rea* requirement more narrowly than the lower courts. Similarly, in *Snyder v. Phelps* (2011) (Roberts), the Court touched on the harmful effects of an exceptionally mean-spirited internet commentary before deciding that the question was not properly before it in that case. **Thus, the Court appears to recognize that the internet expands the impact of and audience for threats, but has decided not to weigh them in making First Amendment doctrine. Old doctrine applies to new technology.**

C. Defamation

The effect of the internet and other electronic media on defamation is much like the effect on threats. The internet encourages unfiltered off-the-cuff assertions, then makes them available throughout the world, and there is no effective method of expunging lies from cyberspace. These aspects add to the harmful effects of traditional defamation, and probably increase damages in individual cases. They do not, however, change the constitutional limits on defamation actions. **Therefore, the First Amendment limitations on defamation addressed in chapter 2 apply without substantial difference in cases involving defamation published on the internet.**

Quite a few cases have considered defamation or related claims concerning internet postings or email. Typical settings for defamation cases are teenage angst, business disputes, and making fun of schoolteachers and administrators. In essence, the internet just provides a new forum, now with international impact, of what used to be letter-writing campaigns, anonymous hall posters, and unending phone calls. Here are a few examples. In *Sanders v. Walsh* (California, 2013), the court considered defamation claims after complaints of shady wig-selling practices proceeded to small claims court, with rebuttals and sur-rebuttals at an online "reputation restorer," Yelp, and a website for merchants to share information about troublesome customers. In another case, a devastating Google review of a wedding venue at Dancing Deer Mountain in Oregon resulted in defamation and intentional interference with economic relations claims (*Newman v. Liles*, Oregon, 2014). One more case involved a student who was suspended for creating a phony MySpace page and posting what the court called "crude content and vulgar language . . . including shameful personal attacks" on her school's principal (*J.S. v. Blue Mountain School District*, 3rd Cir. 2011). Finally, a defamation and emotional distress case resulted from a 13-year-old's creation of a Facebook page for a classmate that contained racially and sexually offensive comments (with allegations of illegal drug use thrown in for good measure), and then inviting many of the victim's friends and teachers to become

Facebook friends of the new account (*Boston v. Athearn*, Georgia, 2014).

While many of these cases simply reflect new opportunities for cranky consumers or naughty juveniles, others reflect very serious conflicts. For example, in *Batzel v. Smith* (9th Cir. 2003), a person who worked in the plaintiff's home discovered what he claimed was artwork stolen by the Nazis. He sent an email reporting his suspicion to a museum security organization. The email was then forwarded to a listserv read by law enforcement and private security officers around the world. *Batzel* addresses one way in which the internet has actually reduced defamation liability. This is through section 230(c) of the Telecommunications Act of 1996, which provides that internet service providers are immune from defamation or obscenity claims as long as they simply republish or distribute content provided by others. This differs from the status of traditional publishers, who are liable for what they choose to publish. Congress apparently concluded that immunity was needed to protect the then-new internet from destructive lawsuits. Thus, the one clear example of substantive law changed by the internet is statutory rather than constitutional, and trims back rather than expands liability. **But still, there is no definitive new rule; in the absence of new rules, traditional (old) First Amendment doctrine applies.**

D. Violent Imagery

There has been a long and robust debate about violent content in movies, television shows, and graphic novels. One view compares violent content to sexual content, and concludes that children should be protected from violent imagery for the same reasons they should be protected from sexual imagery. Notwithstanding the controversy, there has never been a successful movement to prevent violence from being shown in entertainment media. In fact, most often the analogy of violence to sex was used to argue in favor of allowing more access to sexual images rather than less access to violent ones. Still, broadcasters and filmmakers have used voluntary industry rating systems to inform parents of violent as well as sexual content in entertainment.

In the video gaming industry, the effort went beyond the informational approach of voluntary ratings. A 2005 California law prohibited the sale or rental of violent video games to persons under 18 and required labeling to make sure that adults purchasing games for their children could readily determine the nature of the content. The statute was structured to ensure that the restriction would not prevent children from accessing games with a strong literary content (perhaps a first-person sword-wielder version of *The Iliad??*). In this and other features, the California law largely followed the structure of obscenity law. Still, the video game law clearly went *beyond* existing law in prohibiting minors from obtaining games depicting murder, sexual assault, and other criminal conduct in ways that are patently offensive yet alluring to minors.

The Supreme Court struck down the law in *Brown v. Entertainment Merchants Association* (2011) (Scalia). **What's the Takeaway? The majority refused to treat *violent* content as the same as *obscene* content, and held that the video game restrictions could not satisfy Strict Scrutiny.** The case dealt with video games, which at the time were sold and rented primarily on disks. One reason why we read this is not just for its limited holding, but also to look ahead. **Thus, with online gaming being increasingly common, the opinion logically applies to internet access to games, as well as to games on disks or other software.**

In a concurring opinion, Justice Alito noted some of the unique aspects of violent content in new media:

> [Players] have an unprecedented ability to participate in the events that take place in the virtual

worlds that these games create. Players can create their own video-game characters and can use photos to produce characters that closely resemble actual people. . . . In addition, the means by which players control the action in video games now bear a closer relationship to the means by which people control action in the real world. . . . For example, a player who wants a video-game character to swing a baseball bat—either to hit a ball or smash a skull—could bring that about by simulating the motion of actually swinging a bat.

And later:

In some of these games, the violence is astounding. Victims by the dozens are killed with every imaginable implement, including machine guns, shotguns, clubs, hammers, axes, swords, and chainsaws. Victims are dismembered, decapitated, disemboweled, set on fire, and chopped into little pieces. They cry out in agony and beg for mercy. Blood gushes, splatters, and pools. Severed body parts and gobs of human remains are graphically shown.

In all, four of the justices wrote separately to weigh in on the fact that electronic gaming presents dangers to society that justify expanding state power to limit access to such material. As stated by Justice Alito: "When all of the characteristics of video games are taken into account, there is certainly a reasonable basis for thinking that the experience of playing a video game may be quite different from the experience of reading a book, listening to a radio broadcast, or viewing a movie."

The holding in *Brown* is probably most significant for the Court's unwillingness to add violent imagery to the list of exclusions from First Amendment protection. But it also provided an opportunity for the Court to consider the impact of new technology on the First Amendment. As with the other areas discussed above, the **Takeaway** remains: **the Supreme Court to date has not changed First Amendment doctrine in response to electronic media but has instead tried to apply old law to new problems.**

THINGS TO KNOW
• Speech (and other expression) over the internet is fully protected by the First Amendment. • The universal distribution and permanent availability of internet expression has the potential to expand liability and increase damages for threat, defamation, and other speech that can be punished or regulated.

THINGS TO THINK ABOUT
• Should the fact that the internet is readily accessible by children cause courts to rethink whether some violent or sexually explicit material suitable only for adults should be limited online?

CHAPTER 7

Freedom of the Press and Other Enhanced Protections

You may have read that a reporter for a major newspaper refuses to reveal who told her national security secrets. You don't think you could get away with that, but can the reporter? An attorney at the firm where you work told you that he had been ordered by a trial judge not to say anything about an ongoing case, and that the order includes all employees of the firm. Could the judge order a *journalist* not to talk about the case? If the press (whatever *that* means) has special privileges, what are they? Are there other areas that provide enhanced protection for expression, some sort of super-duper Strict Scrutiny?

This chapter addresses three areas in which expression sometimes seems to get extra protection under the First Amendment. The first is the press, which is explicitly included in the protections of the First Amendment. The next is prior restraints, where the government faces extra burdens in challenging speech. Finally, the chapter examines the problem of compelled speech, where government tries to force someone to speak in some fashion.

Here's a **Takeaway** that shows a central theme of this chapter. The First Amendment is very important to the press, but this is less due to the "free press" clause and more due to the fact that much "free speech" law concerns problems faced largely by the press.

A. The Press

What is the press? The contemporary language usage of "press" is probably "the news media." That term includes print publications ranging from serious daily newspapers to lurid weeklies that publish gossip and outright falsehoods, the kind that are sold at grocery store checkout lines. The term also includes organizations unimaginable to the framers, such as the news divisions of broadcast and cable networks, and some unimaginable just two generations ago, such as internet news websites. The term "press" also includes books, which have been published on printing presses since long before the First Amendment was ratified. The Supreme Court has recognized that the press includes "every sort of publication which affords a vehicle of information and opinion." (*Lovell v. City of Griffin* (1938). This probably includes the modern equivalent of the political pamphleteer of the founding period, the amateur blogger.

The First Amendment provides the press with special privileges. After all, it is the only private commercial activity singled out in the Constitution for protection from government oversight. On a more theoretical level, most of what the press does is "speech." Therefore, if there is both freedom of speech *and* freedom of press, freedom of press must add something to freedom of speech, or else there would be no need to mention it.

Not necessarily. Maybe "speech" refers to spoken expression, *literally* speech, with "press" applicable to written expression. Chief Justice Burger wrote in a concurring opinion in *First National Bank of Boston v. Bellotti* (1978) that the framers used the terms interchangeably, but with respect to the different vehicles of expression. This led him to conclude that there was no unique or additional constitutional protection for what he called the institutional press, the book and newspaper businesses (presumably extended even then to include electronic news outlets and now to other electronic formats). Under this view, the language in the First Amendment referring to freedom of the press clarifies that the speech protection includes the institutional press and doesn't provide something extra for the press. Another way of reaching the same conclusion is to interpret the speech clause as the "right," and the reference to the press as a recognition of the primary battleground between government and its critics.

This view has largely prevailed. A word search can find scores of reported cases suggesting one of these theories as a precursor to denying a press claim for protection unavailable to the rest of the public. For example, in *Cohen v. Cowles Media Co.* (1991) (White), the Court held that the First Amendment did not immunize newspapers from a damages action based on a broken promise to keep the identity of a source confidential. The Court emphasized that the press has no immunity from generally applicable laws. Perhaps the best example of this approach in action is *Branzburg v. Hayes* (1972) (White). This was a mirror image of *Cohen,* a claim by news reporters that freedom of the press exempted them from being compelled to provide testimony or other evidence that would reveal confidential sources. The Court saw this as only an "incidental burden" and stated that there is "no special immunity from the application of general laws." It was not equivocal, calling the press claim of a special exemption "reprehensible conduct forbidden to all other persons." *Branzburg* was the death of a credible argument for special First Amendment rights for journalists and reporters. Never again would a media litigator be able to marshal much enthusiasm from the justices for the principle of press immunity.

Branzburg nonetheless contained seeds for some limited press protections that are greater than those available to the rest of the public. While the Court would not infer a reporter's privilege from federal *constitutional* law, it acknowledged that the press could receive such protection from other law. **A majority of states have now adopted "shield" laws that protect reporters and news organizations in state courts.** The *Branzburg* decision itself encouraged this result, as Justice Powell's concurring opinion argued that courts should use a case-by-case balancing test to protect press confidentiality by quashing subpoenas where law enforcement does not have a strong need to obtain information from the press. Since he provided the fifth vote against a constitutional shield, his views reflected the balance of the views on the Court in 1972. Quite a few lower federal courts have fashioned a partial federal press shield along the lines of Justice Powell's approach. Moreover, the Department of Justice adopted regulations that provide that government attorneys may not subpoena reporters to testify except under a showing of substantial need and with approval from the Attorney General. While that is not "Strict Scrutiny," it is both legally and practically a serious limitation on federal prosecutors calling reporters to the witness stand. A somewhat similar pattern can be shown with respect to law enforcement searches. Several years after *Branzburg,* the Court held in *Zurcher v. Stanford Daily* (1978) (White), that newspapers are subject to "generally applicable" Fourth Amendment law, but the case was soon followed by a federal statute that limited newsroom searches by federal law enforcement. A similar pattern of a narrow interpretation of constitutional protection, followed by federal and state legislation to expand protection as a matter of policy, also underlies much of contemporary "free exercise of religion" law, as shown in chapter 8.

Note also that even though the Supreme Court is usually careful to deny special additional rights based on the freedom of

press clause, it is generous in interpreting the freedom of *speech* clause to protect press interests. One of the best examples is defamation law, as discussed in chapter 2. The Supreme Court has on numerous occasions since the 1960s recognized First Amendment speech limits on tort law. While the Court has usually insisted that such protection is not limited to the press, it is hard to imagine many potentially lucrative defamation cases without media defendants. The policies emphasized by the Court in such cases generally surround the public interest in dissemination of newsworthy information. The Supreme Court has also emphasized the heavy burdens of defamation cases on media defendants. **As a practical matter, while it is the free speech clause that imposes limits on defamation claims, it is the press that benefits.**

Florida Star v. B.J.F. (1989) (Marshall) shows the Supreme Court's special concern for the press. This was a civil action based on a statute that allowed recovery *only from media defendants* that reveal the name of a sexual offense victim. The Court borrowed from its defamation cases to conclude that damages may not be awarded where a newspaper lawfully obtains and publishes truthful information about a matter of public significance. The Court was particularly concerned that the statute was not "evenhanded," and imposed liability only on "the media giant." Although the opinion is a stew of ingredients from free speech philosophy, public policy and unique aspects of the Florida statue, the bottom line is quite clear: **free speech requires Strict Scrutiny of such laws, and the press is the apparent beneficiary of the constitutional rule.**

In a somewhat similar fashion, in *Miami Herald Publishing Co. v. Tornillo* (1974) (White), the Supreme Court struck down another Florida statute, one that required newspapers that criticize political candidates to publish replies by those candidates. "Compelling editors or publishers to publish that which 'reason' tells them should not be published" is comparable to "forbidding [the press] to publish specified matter." While private individuals would also presumably be protected from a similar "equal time" requirement, it is hard to imagine a state law imposing the obligation on private individuals. This law, however, intruded into editorial policymaking at Florida newspapers, and the Court's ruling created a right that *as a practical matter* applies only to the press.

Judicial gag orders provide another common setting in which the press is far more likely to take advantage of a speech right. Most gag orders are restraints on revealing confidential or prejudicial information that comes out in litigation. Many cases involve attempts to prevent pre-trial publicity in criminal cases. The media are the logical subjects of such orders, as generally only the press has both motive and means to report such information. In a series of decisions from the mid-1970s to the mid-1980s, the Supreme Court clarified the breadth of the free speech protection from gag orders. In *Nebraska Press Ass'n v. Stuart* (1976) (Burger), a case also discussed in the next section on **prior restraints**, the Court considered a trial court order against reporting confessions and similar evidence in a notorious murder trial. While the Court recognized the need to protect the defendant's right to a fair trial, it limited the availability of such orders in several respects, underscoring both the narrow application of Strict Scrutiny *and* the importance of a free press. Several years later, in *Richmond Newspapers, Inc. v. Virginia* (1980), the Court required that criminal trials must be open to the public, at least absent extraordinarily important interests to the contrary. *Richmond Newspapers* was not rooted in a special freedom for press organizations or reporters, but in the nature of the right to trial by jury. It is not only a press right, but also a public right rooted in the need for oversight of government. The right allows the public, including the press, into criminal cases at all stages. **The primary vehicle for such public oversight of the criminal justice system is almost always through news coverage of criminal cases.** Several later cases clarified this protection (*Richmond Newspapers* had no majority opinion), specifically holding that the right to open trials is based on the First Amendment and protected by case-specific Strict Scrutiny.

The nature and extent of press freedom can be contrasted with that of parties, attorneys, their employees, and courthouse personnel. Such individuals have freedom of speech, but courts have far greater power to gag or otherwise limit release of sensitive information, as the Court held in *Gentile v. State Bar of Nevada* (1991) (Rehnquist). This leads us to what may be considered a sort of combination of a **Takeaway** and an answer to **why we read and discuss these cases: The press does not have a unique First Amendment right *greater* than the general free speech right, but it is the major beneficiary of the general free speech right.**

B. Prior Restraints

One area in which the First Amendment *does* impose an extra-Strict Scrutiny standard involves prior restraints. A prior restraint is what it sounds like: a legal restriction that prevents speech or publication from occurring. Examples include administrative requirements that speakers at an event obtain a license to speak before the event and judicial injunctions against demonstrations, speeches, or book publications. Again, most controversies involve the press. While we are early in this section, it's a good time to ask, **Why do we read and discuss these cases? They help us see and understand that prior restraints were disfavored in the English common law prior to Independence, and one of the major purposes of the First Amendment was to deny the federal government power to restrain speech or otherwise prevent it from occurring.**

The Supreme Court's several leading decisions on prior restraints suggest the typical settings for controversies that involve prior restraints. In 1931, the Supreme Court decided *Near v.*

Minnesota (1931) (Hughes), an appeal from a state court order prohibiting Near and his newspaper, *The Saturday Press,* from publishing any articles accusing Minneapolis officials of corrupt relationships with racketeers. The Supreme Court identified "immunity from previous restraints or censorship" as the central meaning of freedom of the press. It found that the long history of both federal and state governments tolerating vicious press coverage was support for the conclusion that the First Amendment was intended to provide special protection from prior restraints.

Forty years later, the Court decided *New York Times v. United States* (1971) (per curiam). The case involved government suits to enjoin the *Times* and several other newspapers from publishing any portion of "The Pentagon Papers," a voluminous confidential report about the nation's involvement in Vietnam. The material had been leaked to the newspaper by Daniel Ellsberg, a researcher who had worked on the study and who believed that public knowledge of the truth would force the government to change its Vietnam policies. The events and legal wrangling were about as exciting as basic civil procedure can be, with forum shopping, underlying questions about whether a cause of action had been stated, and conflicting court of appeals decisions. Only two weeks went by from the filing of complaints in the district court to the Supreme Court's ruling on the merits. That ruling was a short *per curiam* opinion for six justices stating little more than that the government had not met its "heavy burden of showing justification for the imposition of a [prior] restraint." The opinion was followed by six concurring opinions and three dissenting opinions (a total of ten opinions from a nine justice court!). Given the splintered outcome, it is remarkable anything can be gleaned from the decision.

Notwithstanding that cacophony, we still have a **Takeaway: all of the justices acknowledged that prior restraints may be granted** only in extraordinary cases, and that there is a substantial presumption in all cases *against* prior restraints.

While two justices argued for something approximating an absolute ban on prior restraints, all of the others indicated that there is some room for judicial intervention, with references to the Clear and Present Danger test from *Schenk* (discussed in chapter 2). Several justices seemed open to granting such relief, but only with explicit Congressional authority and standards to guide judicial evaluation of classified information. The dissenters also struck moderate notes, acknowledging the disfavored status of prior restraints, but arguing for judicial power to act temporarily to allow full judicial consideration of the merits. As a result of the fractured opinions, *New York Times* is most important for general principles, such as the *heavy presumption against prior restraints,* and the *overriding practical fact that the government could not meet this burden once the documents were distributed* because a restraint on publication would not be able to undo the harm. Once confidential materials are released, the Humpty Dumpty principle applies, and no remedy is effective. So, here's another **Takeaway: a prior restraint is hard to get, and once the information gets out, a prior restraint serves no purpose.**

That last point has added significance when it is recognized that the Pentagon Papers were physically smuggled out of secure office buildings and copied over a period of weeks and then mailed by U.S. mail to newspapers. Today it takes seconds to download and electronically transmit voluminous records, leading to immediate publication on anonymous websites, possibly before the government even knows anything is missing (see our discussion of Edward Snowden in the previous chapter). This doesn't prevent the government from using espionage or other laws to punish leakers and, in some settings, those who publish confidential information. But, under current law and technology, it is hard to imagine government ever again getting much opportunity to make a case for a prior restraint on publication of materials.

The gag order and open court cases discussed in the previous section illustrate classic judicial reluctance to impose prior restraints. One that is particularly notable is *Nebraska Press Ass'n v. Stuart* (1976) (Burger), in which the Court established a three-part balancing test. **Trial courts asked to ban press reporting about criminal cases must consider:**

> **"1) the nature and extent of pretrial news coverage,**
>
> **2) whether other measures . . . would be likely to mitigate the effects of unrestrained pretrial publicity; and**
>
> **3) how effectively a restraining order would . . . prevent the threatened danger."**

While this looks like a true case-specific balancing test that can come out differently from case to case, the history of the standard in application is that it is a *nearly absolute ban on prior restraints* of news about court proceedings.

In a different setting that avoided the typical procedural burdens of prior restraint, the Court was far more open to prohibiting speech. In the late 1970s, former C.I.A. agent Frank Snepp published a book highly critical of the agency's actions in the final days of the Vietnam War. He never submitted the manuscript to the agency for pre-publication review, as required in an agreement he signed when he joined the agency. In *Snepp v. United States* (1980) (per curiam), the Supreme Court imposed a constructive trust on Snepp and concluded that he was legally barred from publishing the book because of his failure to comply with his contractual obligations. Thus, while the Court is highly reluctant to interpret the First Amendment to allow government to prevent publication generally, it had no similar reservation when the author had contracted away the right to write or speak about a topic.

Snepp, the former C.I.A. officer, was in a position similar to lawyers and others involved in criminal cases who are ordered not to speak publicly about a case in which they are involved. They had a right to free speech, but gave up some of that right as part of their work. Thus, judges may impose gag orders on participants in the criminal justice system, but not on reporters. In theory, the C.I.A. would have been entitled to an injunction against Snepp's book. In fact, however, the book was already in print by the time the government learned about it. Snepp did not profit from his wrongdoing, which may deter the next rogue agent from similarly ignoring the pre-publication review requirement, but the government was not able to get around the practical difficulties of stopping publication once a document is in the hands of third parties. You can buy a copy of Snepp's book any time you want with less than a dozen keystrokes, so the case doesn't provide much of a route to an effective prior restraint.

We have two **Takeaways** for you. First, **the limitations on prior restraints are again rooted in the** *speech* **right and are not limited to the press, but are still of greater significance to the press than to the rest of us.** *Near, New York Times,* and *Stuart* all involved newspapers; *Snepp* involved a book publisher. Second, perhaps because of the Court's failure to render a full opinion in the *New York Times* case, **no decision has restated the applicable standard into modern standard-of-review terminology. It is evident, however, that the test is more demanding than Strict Scrutiny.** So whether you want to borrow from Colonel Sanders and call the standard "Extra Crispy Strict Scrutiny," or from Ronald McDonald and call the standard "Super-sized Strict Scrutiny," it is at least very, very Strict Scrutiny.

C. The Right *Not* to Speak

Most First Amendment controversies focus on people who decide to say something. The text is not that limited, however, referring to the freedom "of" speech, a phrase that logically encompasses *a right not to speak*. A right to silence can also be found in the Fifth Amendment, which is limited to criminal cases, but has taken on a broader cultural meaning from the first part of the Miranda Warnings: "You have the right to remain silent." The Supreme Court has implied that the right is penumbral to the First and Fifth Amendments: "The right to speak and the right to refrain from speaking are components of the broader concept of 'individual freedom of mind.' " **The right not to speak is not absolute, but seems somewhat more protected than the right *to* speak.** (Note that this connects with concepts of the shield of the First Amendment, and the development of the individual that is also promoted by the Amendment.)

The few cases that have charted the right have left only a thin trail of breadcrumbs to locate its boundaries. The leading traditional case on the subject is *West Virginia State Board of Education v. Barnette* (1943) (Jackson). The Court struck down West Virginia's requirement that teachers and students participate in a flag salute at the beginning of the school day, with refusal punishable by expulsion. The requirement was challenged by members of the Jehovah's Witness religion, which believes that national flags are "graven images" prohibited by scripture. Justice Jackson's majority opinion suggests the enhanced scope of the right *not* to speak. It states that censorship is permitted only upon proof of a clear and present danger (see chapter 2), and suggests that *requiring* speech should be permitted only on "even more immediate and urgent grounds." The Court accepted the legitimacy of the law's purpose to express national unity during wartime, but found the means unacceptable, alluding to both ancient and modern attempts to banish dissent by compelling uniform beliefs. The opinion contains one of the most quoted statements about the nature of freedom of expression: "If there is any fixed star in our constitutional constellation, it is that no official, high or petty, can prescribe what shall be orthodox in politics, nationalism, religion, or other matters of opinion." The majority found no justification for compelling this expression, and the dissent was largely relegated to defending the requirement as insignificant because the teachers and students were permitted to disavow their participation in the flag salute.

The Court applied the same principle in an arguably trivial setting when New Hampshire residents challenged that state's requirement that they leave uncovered the state motto, "Live Free or Die," on their license plates (note to students: it is not advisable to restate the motto as "Live Free or Die Hard" on an examination— we have seen it). In *Wooley v. Maynard* (1977) (Burger), the Court overturned a conviction for covering the motto with tape, concluding that requiring owners to display a motto that they found morally objectionable interfered with the right of owners to refrain from speaking, a necessary component of freedom of thought. While states are permitted to use such mottos generally, they must provide an accommodation for dissenters. The use of traditional Strict Scrutiny language undercuts the argument for enhanced protection in this area, but that obscures a key aspect of this controversy. If there is any compelled statement that is universally recognized as formalistic, it is the state motto on license plates. It is hard to imagine that anyone seeing a New Hampshire registered-car would assume the owner believes in "living free or dying." So, **why do we read these cases? The mere fact that the First Amendment right not to speak extends to this speech only remotely associated with the objector reveals the strength of the right.**

Government compels speech in many situations. Subpoenaed witnesses must testify; persons and businesses must file tax and other regulatory documents; and everyone carries around money that depicts symbolic statements as offensive to some as the New Hampshire license plates are to others. This may reflect the presence of compelling interests in some cases and a recognition that the statement will not be attributed to the objectors in others. For example, the Supreme Court upheld a state law requiring private shopping centers to open their property to allow advocacy by outside groups, noting both the public value of encouraging such advocacy and that it was unlikely shoppers would perceive the advocacy to be endorsed by the shopping center owner (*Pruneyard Shopping Center v. Robins* (1980) (Rehnquist)). It similarly upheld a state university activity fee that funded activities opposed by some students (*Board of Regents v. Southworth* (2000) (Kennedy)). On the other hand, the Court held that a St. Patrick's Day Parade could not be required to include parade units that would send a message rejected by the parade's organizers (*Hurley v. Irish-American Gay, Lesbian and Bisexual Group of Boston*) (1995) (Souter) (see chapter 5). This is therefore a dangerous area for making strong statements or confident predictions.

Our **Takeaway: the Court protects the right *not* to speak, at least when it is convinced that the speech will be associated with the objector.** Once someone convinces a court that the government is *making* that person *say something*, the burden of justification falls on the government. As long as the challenger can identify a way to implement an opt-out accommodation that does not affect others, such as simply taping over the license plates as suggested for dissenting New Hampshire residents, there is a good argument that something resembling extra-Strict Scrutiny applies.

THINGS TO KNOW

- Many speech rights, such as limits on defamation and prior restraints, are of particular importance to the press. One result is that news reports and other examples of journalism, perhaps even blogs, receive greater protection than speech in general, but there is no consistent approach.

- There are state and federal statutory protections for the press that expand on First Amendment rights.

- Courts may not "gag" newspapers from reporting on cases, although they may gag individuals involved in the case, such as attorneys and courthouse personnel.

- The government must meet a heavy and possibly unmeetable burden to obtain a prior restraint.

- There is a right *not* to speak that is protected at least as much as the right to speak.

THINGS TO THINK ABOUT

- Freedom of the press was a major reason for the First Amendment, yet current theory provides that the press has no special rights from the Press clause. Why?

- Why such a stark contrast between prior restraints of speech and punishment of speech? If speech is harmful enough to be subject to punishment, why not allow government to prevent it in the first place?

- Why is there a right not to speak, and should it be greater, lesser, or the same as the right to speak?

CHAPTER 8

Free Exercise

You see on the Internet that people in some other parts of the world were executed because they converted to Christianity, and that a traveler to a different nation was arrested for preaching the Bible. You realize that can't happen here. **The reason is the Free Exercise clause.** But what about religious practices most Americans think bizarre, such as handling poisonous snakes, refusing critical medication, or treating women as second class citizens—even committing violence against women—all in the name of religion? Do people get to escape our laws and cultural norms due to their religious beliefs?

A. Nuts and Bolts

There are two religion clauses—the Free Exercise and Establishment Clauses. Both exist to protect religious freedom. That comes as no surprise about the Free Exercise clause, which is (as written) about as straightforward an individual constitutional right as possible.

If your First Amendment class is like most, the religion clauses get second billing and are relegated to the end of the semester. In the Constitution, however, the religion clauses come first. Moreover, **our nation's unique approach to religion may define our dual system of limited government coupled with individual rights as much as, or even more than the freedom of expression. In many ways, that is (early in the chapter)** *why we read and discuss the cases that follow.* One reason for studying the religion clauses is that they reflect that dual structure. The First Amendment prohibits government from establishing religion while <u>simultaneously</u> guaranteeing that government will not interfere with how individuals exercise their religion. How those two clauses interact is potentially a multi-volume treatise. Here, it gets two short (and happy) chapters.

One fundamental question asks **what constitutes religion** for constitutional purposes. This is a typically aggravating constitutional law question because **you know the answer about specific beliefs and groups almost all of the time,** but may have a hard time identifying the critical differences between religions and other social or philosophical movements. Here are some universally accepted *traditional* religions: Christianity (both as one belief system and in its many independent religious denominations, from Methodist to Mormon), Judaism, Islam, Hinduism, and Buddhism. These are the largest and most prevalent in the United States (with the Roman Catholic Church the largest individual denomination), although there are many others. Not too many years ago, the list of common U.S. religions would have stopped after Judaism, which is a warning that application of the religion clauses has to be rethought every few years. From the other direction, many other entities almost certainly do not constitute religions: political parties, Google, the Philadelphia Orchestra Society, the Boy and Girl Scouts, and SEC football. But there are some harder questions in the middle.

Religions typically have a supernatural deity, a god-figure. But this is not necessary, as the Supreme Court recognized in *Torcaso v. Watkins* (1961) (Black). The Court struck down a Maryland law prohibiting persons who would not declare their belief in God from holding public office. The Court's explanation demonstrates the futility of any simple definition of a religion, because included in the Court's description of "religions" were both "Ethical Culture" and "Secular Humanism." If these two philosophies that appear to be rooted in man-made moral belief systems are religions, then other deeply held belief systems may also qualify as religions—science, veganism, and unconditional love of the Boston Red Sox.

During the same era as *Torcaso,* the Supreme Court considered the meaning of religion in several cases involving claims of conscientious objection to military service. The statute establishing the military draft exempted men conscientiously opposed to participation in war because of their "religious training and belief." The Court again rejected the argument that this required a traditional religion or even belief in a Supreme Being, but failed to provide much alternative content other than to conclude that Congress was attempting to distinguish religious beliefs from political choices or personal moral opposition to war. The dodge— and it probably was just that—was to conclude (and this is one early **Takeaway**) that **religion means a sincere and meaningful belief in a deity or system of beliefs that serve a role "parallel to that filled by the orthodox belief in God"** (*United States v. Seeger* (1965)). Call it God or the functional equivalent of a god. While upholding Congress's distinction between religious and personal moral codes, the Court in effect expanded the definition of religion to include many personal moral codes.

In the end, limitations on the ability of courts to define the boundary between philosophy and religion leave the door slightly open. Here's one **Takeaway: One can identify the belief systems** traditionally recognized as religion. Beyond that, one can only look to circumstantial evidence and to statements of persons or groups proclaiming their beliefs to be religious. Any more intrusive inquiry might itself violate the Constitution by passing judgment on the validity of a religious belief. Stated differently, maybe devotion to the Boston Red Sox is a religion . . . as long as someone says it is. Why do we read and discuss this? In some ways it is unsatisfactory regarding our own sense that, all kidding aside, we *know* that the Red Sox aren't religion the same way the Catholic Church is (and remember Boston is one of the most Catholic cities in the country). Plus, in England the "Jedi" faith is widely recognized as a religion, so who knows? But maybe that is part of the challenge—to define *what constitutes religion*, for constitutional purposes in the unusual situation.

B. Belief—The Core Protection of Free Exercise

We can state the basic guarantee of the Free Exercise Clause fairly simply: Government may not interfere with any individual's personal decisions about religion, such as whether to believe in a religion and how to pray. This is clear from the text of the Free Exercise clause, from the history of religion in the United States, and from many Supreme Court precedents over more than 100 years. The Court has often relied on colonial history to tell an oversimplified story along the following lines. Many of the colonies were formed by religious dissenters who objected to limitations on religious freedom in Europe. They saw America as a place where they could worship God as they chose. Different colonies were settled by different groups, and over time, some fell back into a pattern in which government prescribed religious practices. That was unacceptable to the majority of the people, who wrote guarantees of religious freedom into several state constitutions, and then into the First Amendment.

The Supreme Court has often said that **religious freedom is absolute with respect to religious belief.** Thus, a person is free to hold mainstream religious beliefs *or* to hold unusual beliefs that strike most of the public as bizarre, idiotic, or just plain disgusting. Our laws may not punish anyone, even a non-citizen, for worshipping golden idols, convicted con men, Norse Gods, or even the Boston Red Sox (except maybe in the New York City metropolitan area). There are few absolute rights in the Constitution. This is one of them.

United States v. Ballard (1944) (Douglas) shows the almost total lack of government power to challenge religious belief. The government prosecuted a family of preachers for mail fraud, based on their claim to be divine messengers with the power to heal incurable diseases, which they would perform, *for a fee.* The Supreme Court held that the government could not argue that the defendants actually lacked the power to heal—that their religion was false (although it could argue that the defendants did not in fact believe their own claims). In other words, *you can believe anything,* and if you believe what you say, you are immune from prosecution, even if your statements are what the Court admitted was "incredible, if not preposterous, to most people."

What's the Takeaway? Thus, to return to the bizarre practices mentioned in the introductory paragraph, a person may freely *believe* **in the religious significance of snake handling, refusing all medication, and the subjugation of women.**

C. Religious Conduct

With the background of the previous sentence, we have made progress but are not yet done. The clause is more complex than the nice, neat "any belief" branch, for it also protects "exercise," which is an action verb. **The clause protects religious conduct, not just belief or speech.**

Religious conduct is protected, but that protection is not absolute and can be regulated by government in limited circumstances. Fortunately for law students, the constitutional law governing the regulation of religious conduct falls largely into categories familiar from the general Constitutional Law course (and from the previous chapters on speech regulation). These are essentially versions of Strict Scrutiny and Rational Basis Scrutiny. *Unfortunately* for law students, the determination of the appropriate category to apply is sometimes confusing. This is partly because the doctrines in the area are still developing, and partly because laws have changed some of those First Amendment doctrines, essentially outranking federal constitutional law (how does *that* happen?). The rest of this chapter takes a short trip through history to reveal that the extent of legal protection of religious conduct *varies by the nature of the conduct, the type of law involved, and even by the place it occurs.*

1. *The Supreme Court's Decisions Before* Smith

The Supreme Court's earliest decisions considering the scope of the Free Exercise Clause tended to defer to government authority rather than to require tolerance of minority religious practices. Some of these decisions dealt with central moral beliefs, such as *Reynolds v. United States* (1878) (Waite), which held that polygamy based on religious beliefs could be prosecuted as a crime. Others dealt with laws that were less intrusive on religious practices, such as *Braunfeld v. Brown* (1961), in which the Court upheld a Sunday closing law that burdened storeowners who followed a Sabbath other than Sunday.

The next era offered more protection for individual religious practices. The two most important cases were *Sherbert v. Verner* (1963) (Brennan) and *Wisconsin v. Yoder* (1972) (Burger). Sherbert was another Sabbath case. A Seventh Day Adventist lost her job for refusing to work on Saturdays. The state denied unemployment benefits because she was unwilling to accept any other job that required Saturday work. The Court rejected use of the rational basis test because the unemployment compensation law made government benefits depend on a person's violation of a central tenet of her faith. **The Court imposed Strict Scrutiny, requiring that the state establish a "compelling state interest" that "no alternative form of regulation would satisfy." So here's a Takeaway from the case (but don't hang on to it for too long): the state needed a means necessary to achieve a compelling interest.** The state could not satisfy either requirement.

Yoder dealt with a conflict between the Amish practice of ending classroom education at age fourteen and Wisconsin's law (like most states) that required attendance until sixteen. The Court struck down application of the law to the Amish, concluding that the value of education for two additional years did not outweigh the burden imposed on Amish religious practices. Chief Justice Burger's rapturous opinion for the Court suggests that he fell in love with the Amish lifestyle, which perhaps led the majority to overlook some problems in the legal analysis, such as the fact that the educational practices of the Amish were social and economic rather than religious, and may have been related more to a desire to isolate their teenagers from non-Amish peers than to actual religious beliefs. The Court was also vague about the applicable standard of review. The most specific reference in the majority opinion was "only those [State] interests of the highest order and those not otherwise served can overbalance legitimate claims to the free exercise of religion," which most lower courts treated as a reaffirmation of the Strict Scrutiny requirement of *Sherbert*. **What's the Takeaway?** *Sherbert* **and** *Yoder* **were together taken to establish Strict Scrutiny as applicable when a state or federal law infringes on religious practices.**

2. Smith—*A Return to Deference*

The Court signaled a major shift from Strict Scrutiny in *Employment Division v. Smith* (1990) (Scalia), a case involving two members of the Native American Church, which uses the illegal hallucinogenic drug peyote in its rituals. They were not prosecuted, but they were fired from their jobs as drug counselors. They sought unemployment compensation, which was denied on the ground that they had been fired for work-related misconduct. The Supreme Court affirmed the benefits denials in an opinion by Justice Scalia that remains highly controversial today. He wrote that *Sherbert* did not involve a claimant whose dismissal was based on illegal conduct. This fact provided the key to the principle enunciated in *Smith*. **What's the Takeaway? State criminal laws of general applicability are enforceable even where they prevent a person from engaging in religious practices.** The Court cited *Reynolds* (polygamy) and cases dealing with obligations under the child labor and tax laws in support of the principle. **Laws of general applicability need only satisfy minimal scrutiny—a rational connection to a legitimate state objective.**

The majority explained that this rule protects most religious practices. Gathering together for religious services, participating in sacraments, and following religious dietary rules would all remain protected because none of these practices is prohibited by generally applicable laws, and certainly not by criminal laws. The majority then distinguished *Sherbert* and *Yoder,* noting that neither involved a claim of exemption from a criminal prohibition, and describing *Yoder* as one of a number of hybrid cases based on the fundamental right of parents to control the education of their children, in which religion played only some part. This would come as a surprise to the justices who decided *Yoder,* as the majority opinion in that case emphasized that the exemption from compulsory attendance laws was based on religion and explicitly stated that parental control over their children's education was only a basis for recognizing the parental role in the dispute. (Not to mention that the *Yoder* court referred several times to "general applicability" as *not* a basis for upholding application of laws that interfere with religious practices.) The Court also suggested that *Sherbert* should be limited to its particular setting, unemployment compensation.

There are at least two problems with these distinctions. First, some mainstream sacraments are subject to generally applicable criminal laws, but receive exemptions for religious use, such as drinking age laws. Thus, mainstream religions are often able to obtain exceptions for their practices, and the failure to extend accommodations to a minority religion undercuts the entire premise of free exercise. Second, this *was* an unemployment compensation case.

The *Smith* majority opinion left some wiggle room for constitutional protection of religious practices at odds with generally applicable laws. **First, laws directed at religious practices as such are subject to greater than Rational Basis Scrutiny.** (This became clearer after the *Lukumi Babalu Aye* case several years later, as discussed below). **Second, where the religious exercise claim is joined with another constitutional claim, the two claims together can provide a strong enough interest to require Strict Scrutiny (as in the Court's revision of** *Yoder).* The thrust of the opinion was quite clear, however. Strict Scrutiny of laws affecting religious practices would result in "religious exemption from civic obligations of almost every conceivable kind," citing laws in numerous areas and unintentionally foreshadowing debates about employer health insurance mandates and same-sex marriage 25 years later.

To keep things short and happy, we do not engage here in extended debates about the importance of non-majority opinions. Still, you should note that the majority opinion was extremely controversial from the start. Justice O'Connor wrote a blistering concurring opinion in which she agreed that compensation could be denied, but rejected the "generally applicable" premise as irrelevant. She joined the judgment only because she concluded that the Oregon decision to deny benefits withstood Strict Scrutiny. Three other justices dissented on several grounds, indicating that this was a closer case than the typically confident Scalia opinion suggested. Nevertheless, *Smith* has never been overruled. The next two sections, however, suggest major limitations on its application.

D. Limiting *Smith*—Laws Directed at Religious Practices

Three years after *Smith*, the Supreme Court decided *Church of the Lukumi Babalu Aye, Inc. v. City of Hialeah* (1993) (Kennedy). The Court struck down ordinances that prohibited the Santeria religion's ritual practice of animal sacrifice. Many longtime residents of Hialeah did not want a Santeria church in the city and persuaded the city council to adopt a series of ordinances based on the police power interest in preventing animal cruelty. In abstract form, the city's ordinances were generally applicable—no one was permitted to "sacrifice" animals. In addition, killing for food (which was required by Santeria practice) was explicitly prohibited unless conducted using methods prescribed by the city that were incompatible with Santeria ritual. As a practical matter the requirements gerrymandered Santeria out of Hialeah while burdening no one else because the city enacted exceptions that allowed killing animals for pretty much any reason *other* than Santeria ritual sacrifice. For example, the ordinances specifically allowed kosher killing, thereby preferring one religious practice to another (a likely Establishment Clause issue, as shown in the next chapter).

The Supreme Court reaffirmed *Smith* but stressed that (here's a **Takeaway**) **the general applicability requirement applies to the** *purpose* **of a law as well as to its application to all persons.** Laws *intended* to burden religious practices are discriminatory, in contrast to laws such as the peyote prohibition in *Smith*, which was applicable to all persons, and had only a *collateral effect* of burdening members of the Native American Church. Justice Kennedy's majority opinion in *Lukumi* stated "[I]f the object of a law is to infringe upon or restrict practices because of their religious motivation, the law is not neutral." **Why do we read and discuss this? Like some free speech case law we have looked at, the Court here cares about the** *intent* **of the law. Strict Scrutiny applies when the motivation of a law is hostility to a religious practice.**

The Court found that while prohibiting animal cruelty would be a permissible objective, the city's choice to prohibit only animal cruelty committed in certain religious practices was both discriminatory against religion (thereby undercutting the "compelling interest" requirement) and a seriously underinclusive method of achieving the interest (thereby failing the means portion of the test). All nine justices agreed with the outcome, with several emphasizing the fact that discriminating against religious practices is *per se* unconstitutional.

Lukumi Babalu Aye has been read as narrowing the broad implications of *Smith* that laws of general application receive no extra judicial scrutiny. The case should eliminate one of the dire predictions by opponents of *Smith*, that governments would be free to pass "generally applicable" laws intended to burden minority religions practices. Still, the evidence of the anti-Santeria motivation in this case was strong, and the terms of the ordinances made clear that they were "generally applicable" only in a very broad sense of the term. **What's the Takeaway?** *Lukumi Babalu Aye* **therefore stands largely as a strong symbolic statement** against anti-religious motivation, but can probably be distinguished in most cases that deal with truly "generally applicable" laws. And why do we read this? Both to understand the analysis of free exercise cases, *and* to see how motivation can be important to Court analysis, here and elsewhere.

E. Congress and the States Respond

Also in 1993, Congress passed the Religious Freedom Restoration Act ("RFRA"), which explicitly reinstated the Strict Scrutiny standard for federal, state, and local laws. **The Act provides that whenever a law "substantially burdens" a religious practice, it may not be applied unless it satisfies the "compelling interest" test—in effect, Strict Scrutiny.** The statute may be read as a rebuke to the *Smith* Court for failing to provide adequate protection for religious practices. The law was held unconstitutional with respect to state and local governments in *City of Boerne v. Flores* (1997) (Kennedy). Here the Supreme Court concluded that Congress lacked authority under the 14th Amendment's enforcement clause to regulate state and local laws burdening religion. The Act was later upheld, however, with respect to *federal laws*. This became the center of controversy in 2014. In *Burwell v. Hobby Lobby Stores, Inc.,* (2014) (Alito), the Supreme Court enforced RFRA to require that the government grant exceptions from provisions of the Affordable Care Act mandate that employers provide health insurance for employees where that action was incompatible with the religious beliefs of the owners. The Court noted that a federal "action that imposes a substantial burden on religious exercise must serve a compelling government interest, and . . . must also constitute the least restrictive means of serving that interest." *Hobby Lobby* presented a number of issues that pushed "culture war" buttons, such as whether corporations have religious beliefs and the potential application of the law to religious practices at odds with dominant social views, such as equal treatment based on gender, sexual orientation, and race. At a minimum, *Hobby Lobby* signals a vigorous application of RFRA to protect practices rooted in religious beliefs. Our **Takeaway** brings us full circle: **As a matter of federal statutory law, the Strict Scrutiny standard of *Sherbert* and *Yoder* is** again **"good law" with respect the federal government.**

In 2000 Congress again acted to protect free exercise at the state and local level in the Religious Land Use and Institutionalized Persons Act. This statute required governments to satisfy Strict Scrutiny whenever their actions in either of these two areas "substantially burden" religious practices. There is a long history of conflicts between state and local land use regulations and prison rules on one side and individual religious practices on the other. In *Cutter v. Wilkinson,* (2004) (Ginsburg), a case concerning religious rights of state prisoners, the Court upheld the law, finding that Congress avoided the flaw of RFRA by using its interstate commerce and spending powers. No land use case has made its way to the Supreme Court, but there is no reason to expect a different outcome concerning that portion of the law. Thus, in these two major areas of state law, protection of religious practices reverted to Strict Scrutiny as a matter of federal statutory law.

Many states similarly reacted to *Smith* by mandating greater protection of religious practices. **Some states did so by interpreting their own constitutions to require Strict Scrutiny. Others did so by legislation.** While not all states have acted, and thus disputes *other* than those involving land use or institutionalized persons remain subject to *Smith,* a majority of states have joined with Congress in imposing *greater restrictions on government,* therefore providing *more legal protection for religious practices.*

F.　Stable Law

Chapter **Takeaway:** Despite the back and forth between the Supreme Court and Congress over the appropriate standard of review for laws that burden religious practices, the law in this area is generally stable, although not uniform from state to state. Religious beliefs are absolutely protected, and in most respects laws that "substantially burden" religious practices are valid only where they satisfy Strict Scrutiny. The fact that much of this is due to state law means that religious practices are more protected in some states than others, but there seems to be no trend toward repealing such protections, and they are probably here to stay. In areas untouched by federal or state religious freedom restoration acts, many laws that are truly generally applicable are not subject to any special free exercise limitations.

So what of the unusual religious practices mentioned at the beginning of this chapter? Laws that prohibit snake-handling would seem to be valid as "generally applicable safety laws", unless a challenger can make a showing, as in the *Lukumi Babalu Aye* case, that the ban was directed at *religions* that use snakes in their rituals. Even then, such bans may satisfy the demands of Strict Scrutiny. Laws requiring use of life-saving medication constitute more of a problem. *Smith* might appear to allow such laws, but there are non-First Amendment constitutional protections of bodily autonomy that allow people to reject unwanted medical treatment (remember that Fourteenth Amendment discussion from Con Law?). Thus, such laws probably fall within *Smith*'s interpretation of *Yoder* and would be unenforceable. Religious practices that treat women as second-class citizens also raise complex issues. Most such practices would likely violate generally applicable equal rights laws, unless either the Free Exercise Clause or the equal rights statute requires an exception for religious discrimination. For example, religions are allowed to reserve the priesthood for men. On the other hand, violence against women would be against the law under any standard of review, even if it is rooted in religious doctrine. It is probably an example of a situation in which American society would agree that *Smith* should apply.

THINGS TO KNOW

- The freedom of religious belief is absolute.

- The freedom of religious conduct is more complex. Strict Scrutiny applies in cases of laws directed at religious practices and where laws also inhibit the exercise of other constitutional rights. As a matter of statutory law, Strict Scrutiny applies to federal laws that substantially burden religious practices and to state and local laws concerning land use or institutionalized persons. Many states have constitutional or statutory law that requires Strict Scrutiny of all government action that substantially burdens religious practices. In other words, Rational Basis Scrutiny applies as a matter of constitutional law for truly "generally applicable" laws. **Yuck, is this complicated!**

THINGS TO THINK ABOUT

- Why is this structure so convoluted?

- Was *Smith* correct to assert a general rule, or should it have been presented as either an exception to Strict Scrutiny or an application of Strict Scrutiny that the state law satisfies?

- Will the *Hobby Lobby* ruling result in a re-examination of the balance between government power to regulate and its obligation to accommodate dissenting religious practices?

CHAPTER 9

Establishment Clause

A. The Relationship to Free Exercise

The Establishment Clause differs from the Free Exercise Clause in critical ways. The basic purpose of each clause is the same—to enhance religious freedom—but the methods are polar opposites. **While the Free Exercise Clause allows almost all religious activities, the Establishment Clause prohibits government support of many of those same religious activities.** Practical effects of this distinction are 1) persons attempting to enforce the Establishment Clause often find themselves in conflict with organized religions and 2) religious groups often disagree among themselves about the application of the clause to specific government activities. Free exercise is a Santa Clause bag that never runs out of presents, so most people see it as a no-strings-attached benefit. Establishment, on the other hand, is a tightly budgeted Christmas list. If someone receives, someone else loses. Sometimes the loser is a deeply religious person and sometimes the loser is an atheist. This fact alone makes generalizations about the nature of Establishment Clause conflicts risky.

A second key distinction may be more an historical accident of shifting Supreme Court majorities than principled constitutional interpretation. **While most free exercise cases can be resolved with reference to broad principles, such as "generally applicable laws" or "Strict Scrutiny," establishment cases have developed their own unique doctrines, many of them useless outside of a narrow range of facts.** This then is bad news for law students, because it takes more effort to learn establishment than to learn free exercise. For lawyers, however, this is good news, because they will find more room to make arguments on behalf of their clients.

An important lesson for law students is to look for ways in which the two clauses complement each other. In most other areas, a constitutional "right" draws a line between government power and individual liberty. Government cannot unreasonably search, impose excessive bail, or censor most speech. Government may, however, act cautiously and decide *not* to search, impose *no* bail condition, or allow *all* speech. While the decision may be unwise or bad politics, governments can usually avoid violating the Constitution simply by staying away from the line, or to mix metaphors, by backing away from the edge of the cliff. Similar risk-averse behavior is rarely possible with the religion clauses. When government moves back from a cliff edge relating to religion, it generally just moves toward another cliff. **If government wants to make sure it respects free exercise, it runs the danger of violating establishment, and vice versa.** For example, if government steps back from the line to protect free exercise, it may retreat too far and establish religion, perhaps by providing benefits to religious groups that are unavailable to non-religious ones. From the other direction, if government focuses too heavily on its duty not to establish religion, it may unintentionally deny full free exercise rights by denying required accommodations.

Trying to answer questions about how to define religion or the relationship between the First Amendment's religion clauses is like walking a tightrope. But we will (borrowing from the literature on business management) recast this challenge as an opportunity. It's hard to be wrong when the questions are so amorphous. **But it hurts to fall off the tightrope, and anyone who purports to predict with much accuracy the outcome of religion clause cases risks being seen as a liar or a fool.**

B. The Core Doctrine

We can start with a mini-**Takeaway: at a minimum, the Establishment Clause prevents the federal government from recognizing a religion as the nation's official religion.** If that is all it means (and that's all Justice Thomas thinks it means), this would be a simple chapter. And we *do* want this to be short and happy. But it's not so simple; even if that was the original intent, the Establishment Clause has become much more than that. Establishment has morphed to mean something akin to "favor," so think of the general rule as stating that **government may not favor one religion over other religions (or even non-religion).**

Much of the law in this area is based on the case *Lemon v. Kurtzman* (1971) (Burger). The Court reviewed statutes from Pennsylvania and Rhode Island that provided public funding for some private school teachers. The state laws were complex, but each provided salary supplements for teachers of secular subjects as a financial incentive for good teachers to remain in the profession. The laws were crafted to avoid supporting religious teaching or to give private school teachers any advantage over public school teachers. The Court nevertheless struck down the laws under the Establishment Clause. It found the following requirements from prior cases. **A state law:**

- "must have a secular legislative purpose,"

- must have a "principal or primary effect that neither advances nor or inhibits religion,"

  and

- "must not foster an excessive government entanglement with religion."

The salary supplements had a good "secular" purpose (better teaching), and the Court never resolved the second issue. It concluded, however, that the state programs inevitably required too much entanglement of government and religion. The states would have to audit the books and otherwise oversee the operation of religious schools to make sure that public funds were not used for religious education.

Here's the **Takeaway:** *Lemon* **purports to establish a clear rule: a law challenged under the Establishment Clause must satisfy** *each* **of the three requirements: secular purpose, "non-religious" primary effect, and no excessive entanglement.** The case remains "good" law, but its helpfulness in some settings is doubtful. First, Supreme Court majorities have ignored *Lemon* on a number of occasions. Second, even when using the *Lemon* test, justices seem aware of its deficiencies, rendering it an unreliable foundation for an Establishment Clause challenge. Third (perhaps this is the reason why the test survives despite the many criticisms), the test is malleable. This renders it less useful generally than it was in *Lemon*. Most laws can be found to have at least one valid secular purpose, so the first requirement is fairly weak. Second, it is very common for parties and justices to disagree about the principal or primary effects of government practices. Third, how much *entanglement* does it take to be *excessive*? It is easy to suspect that supporters of a challenged government program will find a secular purpose, non-religious primary effect, and comparatively little entanglement, and opponents will find the reverse. But you've already gotten this far in Constitutional Law, so this should come as no surprise.

Attempts to replace *Lemon* with other tests, such as Justice O'Connor's reliance on "endorsement" and Justice Kennedy's emphasis on "coercion," have also failed as universal tests. The *Lemon* test at least provides a good general starting point for identifying relevant issues. As this chapter reveals, Supreme Court majorities still rely on *Lemon* when they choose to do so, and ignore it just as readily when that is their preference. Justice Scalia has deplored the decision, comparing it to a "ghoul in a late-night horror movie" that frightens "little children." (Does it surprise you that Justice Scalia would use over-the-top language to describe a case that has been cited in dozens of cases over forty years by most of his colleagues? Maybe not.)

C. Different Settings, Rules, and Outcomes

When Establishment Clause cases are organized into typical settings, some patterns emerge. These allow lawyers to make predictions, although they cannot be wholly reliable. We look at four settings and the rules they establish.

1. Religion in Public Schools

One example concerns religious activities in public schools. Courts are *most* likely to find that the official inclusion of religion in public school classes and events crosses the establishment line. Two important cases were decided by the Supreme Court in the early 1960s. *Engel v. Vitale* (1962) (Black) considered a challenge to New York State's official nondenominational prayer for use at public school functions. The other, *Abington School District v. Schempp* (Clark) (1962), involved mandatory Bible readings in public elementary schools. The decisions concluded that the *official use* of religious texts, at least in elementary schools, adds up to unconstitutional religious indoctrination. New York's prayer may have been nondenominational, but it was still a *prayer*. The Court stated: "Religion is too personal, too sacred, too holy, to permit its 'unhallowed perversion' " by government. While the state prayer did not elevate one religion over others, it officially made religion a part of compulsory public education. The Bible readings in *Schempp* more obviously elevated some religions over others, and the Court emphasized the need to "maintain strict neutrality, neither aiding nor opposing religion." (These two decisions were among the most influential in galvanizing opposition to the Warren Court; "Impeach Earl Warren" became a common roadside sign in the 1960s, especially in deep southern states and the Bible belt.)

The spiritual heirs of these cases were decided many years later. In *Lee v. Weisman* (1992) (Kennedy), the Supreme Court considered the constitutionality of prayers at a middle school graduation ceremony. Justice Kennedy's majority opinion concluded that religious prayers at such events violate the Establishment Clause, even though the specific prayers in question were ecumenical, like the New York State prayer in *Engel*. Justice Kennedy viewed the critical issue as *coercion*. **What's the Takeaway? Because a graduation ceremony is the culmination of the academic year, and students should not be expected to forego attendance for reasons of conscience, the use of prayers compelled participation in religious activities (at least as a practical matter), and that violates the Establishment Clause.** One aspect of *Lee* that supporters of a greater role for religion in public schools seized upon was the Court's emphasis on the fact that the *school*, rather than students, arranged for the graduation speakers. This led many school districts to stop arranging for graduation prayers and to instead direct students to plan programs, including prayer only if the students chose to do so. When a challenge to this practice made its way to the Supreme Court, the justices did not find that distinction sufficient to broadly validate student prayers. In *Santa Fe Independent School District v. Doe* (2000) (Stevens), the Court confronted student-arranged (and led) prayers before high school football games. The Court concluded that the district's policy at least implicitly endorsed religion, and that was sufficient to convince a majority that it established religion. Thus, **why read *both these cases?* Because public education is to be free of publicly sponsored or encouraged religious content through high school.**

Two important cases decided in the 1980s applied *Lemon* to invalidate less overtly religious practices. In *Wallace v. Jaffree* (1985) (Stevens), the Court struck down a "moment of silence" law, even though the law itself made no direct reference to religion. A majority concluded, however, that legislative history confirmed that the law's *purpose* was to encourage prayer in public schools. Ironically, this reliance on the first prong of the *Lemon* test provided a blueprint for enacting valid laws requiring moments of silence: cut out the religion in official statements about the purposes of the law. This satisfies prong one, and moments of silence are now generally upheld, as many thousands of Millennials can testify based on their elementary and high school experiences.

In a more important decision also based on the "secular purpose" requirement of *Lemon*, the Court struck down a Louisiana law that that required the teaching of "creation science" in biology classes. In *Edwards v. Aguillard* (1987) (Brennan), the Court concluded that "creation science" is religion rather than science, noting "we need not be blind in this case to the legislature's preeminent religious purpose in enacting this statute." On a micro-level, responses to the decision have included numerous attempts to include in public school curriculums versions of similar theories under scientific-sounding names, such as "intelligent design." These attempts have generally failed, with courts holding such requirements to violate the Establishment Clause. On a macro-level, *Edwards* began a still-ongoing battle about whether the teaching of science and other academic subjects that reject the beliefs of some religious groups "establishes" secular humanism, science, or perhaps simply "anti-religion," and as a result teaching such subjects would also be unconstitutional.

2. Government Support of Religious Education

The converse of religious content in public education would seem to be official involvement in religious education. A strong "wall of separation" theory would seem likely to treat the two areas as similar and be wary of permitting any connection. That has not been the case, however, as **the Supreme Court has expressed far less concern about government support than it has about religion in public schools.** A good example is *Everson v. Board of Education* (1947) (Black), the first modern establishment case. The suit challenged the local board of education's decision to provide parents with free transportation to their children's school, regardless of whether it was public or private, including religious schools. While Justice Black's opinion set out the Court's "official history" of church-state relations (see chapter 8) and reinvigorated Thomas Jefferson's "wall of separation" metaphor, a majority upheld the public support in question. The public funds were used for the non-religious purpose of transportation, the funds went directly to families rather than to religious schools, and the funds were spent in a neutral fashion—they were provided for transportation to all schools, public, secular private, and religious private. Justice Black's opinion included a list of Establishment Clause rules that is still largely accurate today:

> The 'establishment of religion' clause of the First Amendment means at least this: Neither a state nor the Federal Government can set up a church. Neither can pass

laws, which aid one religion, aid all religions, or prefer one religion over another. Neither can force nor influence a person to go to or to remain away from church against his will or force him to profess a belief or disbelief in any religion. No person can be punished for entertaining or professing religious beliefs or disbeliefs, for church attendance or non-attendance. No tax in any amount, large or small, can be levied to support any religious activities or institutions, whatever they may be called, or whatever form they may adopt to teach or practice religion. Neither a state nor the Federal Government can, openly or secretly, participate in the affairs of any religious organizations or groups and vice versa.

Lemon was a "support for religious schools" case that went the other way. There are several important differences from *Everson*. One obvious difference is that the funds in *Lemon* went directly to the private schools. Another was that the interaction of the specific rules governing state payments and the practicalities of the availability and cost of private education in the two states meant that the benefits were provided almost entirely to parochial schools. After *Lemon,* the Supreme Court considered numerous cases involving some form of public support for parochial education, but appeared to reach no meaningful consensus or coherent rule. Senator Daniel Patrick Moynihan of New York once derided the Court for developing a doctrine in which government could provide books but not maps, and then asked which rule applied to atlases. It is probably fair to characterize these cases as experimenting with appropriate boundaries, and to treat the sometimes inconsistent results as due to changes of the Court's membership as much to the malleable quality of the *Lemon* test.

In recent years, the Court has consistently shown greater willingness to approve public financial support of religious

schools. In *Agostini v. Felton* (1997) (O'Connor), the Court overruled a prior decision that struck down New York State's practice of sending special education teachers to work with students at parochial schools. The earlier decision found that the state was subsidizing religious education because by it freed church funds from supporting special education (which allowed the schools to advance religion with the savings) and because the presence of public school teachers in parochial schools and necessary monitoring constituted excess entanglement similar to that in *Lemon*. By 1997, a very different majority decided that any advancement of religion was sufficiently indirect to avoid constitutional concerns and that "extensive monitoring" was not necessary. It pointed out that (here's your **Takeaway**) the Court has "always tolerated some level of involvement between" church and state. **Why do we read and discuss this?** To consider whether this was a factually distinguishable situation, or just a matter of different justices with different attitudes? It doesn't really matter, but you should read both and make up your own mind.

Two more cases show the Court's willingness to interpret *Lemon* in a more generous fashion than most earlier parochial school aid cases. In *Mitchell v. Helms* (1999), the Court upheld a federal spending program that allocated funds for school supplies to parochial as well as to public and secular private schools. The Court rejected the artificial distinctions of the "map" cases, but was unable to reach a majority ruling on the applicable doctrine. This is what we call a *scorecard decision*, where you need a scorecard to keep track of what they said and what it means. A four-justice plurality concluded that the spending program was consistent with *Everson's* emphasis on neutrality, and treated as immaterial the fact that some funds were clearly used to advance religion, thereby choosing not to follow part two of the *Lemon* test. The rest of the Court was unwilling to jettison *Lemon*. *Two* justices concluded that the spending program was valid under *Lemon* because any advancement of religion was trivial, and *three* justices would apply *Lemon* to overturn the law. Thus, seven justices at least seemed to believe that the *Lemon* test disallowed the federal aid in question, and five justices treated *Lemon* as the governing precedent, but there were still six votes to uphold the aid program. Some very mind-bending scholarship examines how this sort of anomalous legal analysis occurs. It sometimes makes our job more fun and always makes your job more difficult.

Zelman v. Simmons-Harris (Rehnquist) (2002) may suggest a similar breakdown of views with a clearer outcome. The issue before the Court was Ohio's school voucher program, which provided public funds to allow students in underperforming school districts in Cleveland to pay tuition and then enroll at better schools. The program was clearly designed to improve non-religious education, which satisfied all nine justices on the first prong of the *Lemon* test. A majority found the law valid under prongs two and three as well. The program was complex, but was rooted in parental choice and did not favor placements in religious schools in theory. The majority emphasized that the "program was entirely neutral with respect to religion" (it actually favored public school placements over religious school placements). In fact, however, no suburban public schools elected to participate, meaning that most vouchers were used at religious schools. This fact drove the division on the Court, with five justices finding that the neutral and "market driven" aspects (along with less concern than thirty years earlier about the entanglement resulting from audits) rendered the program constitutional, and four justices finding that because the overwhelming number of schools receiving public funding in this fashion were religious, the Ohio plan crossed the line and established religion.

There is a clear **Takeaway** here. **At least for the foreseeable future, the Court is likely to uphold public support of parochial** education (and other religious schools), if three facts are present:

- parents direct the funds,

- the funds are used to support teaching secular subjects *(i.e.,* the same courses taught in public schools),

- the funds are distributed neutrally, that is, equally available to non-religious private schools as well as to religious schools.

Why do we read and discuss this? These cases raise questions of how we interpret what the Court does, and why it does what it does. Polls suggest that a substantial portion of the public supports such programs, concluding that they improve education more than they support religion. Perhaps the answer is simply that "the Supreme Court follows the election returns." The views of the justices on at least some legal questions seem to be influenced by what they perceive to be a public consensus.

3. *Prayer at Government Functions*

Some of the trickiest Establishment Clause problems concern actions by government that acknowledge religion or suggest support for a religious belief (in this country this is almost always Christianity). Here are some of the reasons. First, many of these practices pre-date the relatively recent conclusion that the Establishment Clause extends to state and local government. Is the long history of such practices support for their continuation or evidence that they are relics of the past? Second, some of these practices seem formal, largely devoid of actual religious sentiment. Does that mean they are so unimportant they cannot "establish," or does it instead mean that they cannot be justified? Third, some of the most overtly religious expressions by government remain immune to litigation (how would *you* like to be the Scrooge who challenges the government's designation of an official holiday called Christmas?). Is that a failing of our judicial system or just recognition that actual injury is necessary for there to be a constitutional violation?

In *Marsh v. Chambers* (1983) (Burger), the Supreme Court considered the constitutionality of a state legislature's employment of a chaplain, who gave opening prayers at daily legislative sessions. The Court upheld the practice, declining to use the *Lemon* test, and instead emphasizing the long tradition of such officers and practices. The Court stated: "To invoke Divine guidance on a public body entrusted with making the laws is not" establishment, but rather "a tolerable acknowledgment of beliefs widely held among the people of this country." Some commentators noted the ritualistic nature of religion at public ceremonies, concluding that the religious components are unimportant and that no one seriously thinks they indicate that the government actually supports the religious beliefs expressed in ceremonies.

A challenge to that view came before the Supreme Court in 2014 in *Town of Greece v. Galloway* (2014) (Kennedy). The town began its monthly board meetings with invocations by local members of the clergy. Some prayers were overtly sectarian; others were more ecumenical. After complaints that the invocations were always Christian, the town board invited Jewish, Baha'i, and even Wiccan (!) speakers. The majority did not apply the *Lemon* test, and instead found a public value in incorporating a religious component into public meetings and placed Greece's practice within the "traditional" category identified in *Marsh* (even though Greece had used religious invocations only since 1999). The most significant aspect of the decision may be that the sectarian nature of some of the prayers was turned into a virtue. The Court concluded that the range of prayers represented the community, especially as the town's officials encouraged participation by all local religious groups, including atheists. If the Town were to pre-approve the prayers, it would be acting "as supervisors and censors of religious speech, [which] would involve government in religious matters to a far greater degree than is the case under the town's current practice." The Court stated that once a government allows prayers, it may not limit the religious speech to ecumenical prayers, or else it would cross over to violating the Free Exercise Clause. This is a good example of the narrow tightrope between the two clauses, leading us to another **Takeaway:** *Town of Greece* **strengthens government's ceremonial power to include religion in public life, at least as long as the religion is directed at adults.**

4. *Religious Symbolism*

The Court has regularly looked to history and context to uphold religious symbolism. The year after *Marsh,* the Court considered *Lynch v. Donnelly* (1984) (Burger), a challenge to a city's annual outdoor Christmas display, which included a crèche along with items associated with Christmas, such as colored lights, a decorated tree, and a Santa Claus. A majority concluded that the display was largely seasonal, recognizing historical events and including non-religious pagan customs, and was therefore not in violation of the Establishment Clause. Justice O'Connor concurred in an opinion that emphasized her endorsement theory. She was less impressed with the historical justification than with the fact that the presence of numerous non-religious symbols communicated that the city was acknowledging celebrations of the end of the year rather than endorsing the religious meaning of Christmas. The guiding principle of the decision was uncertain. Was it a sort of "historical pageantry may include religious themes" ruling, or was it instead a "context renders the religious component trivial" ruling? A similar issue arose a few years later, when the Court considered two holiday displays in public areas in Pittsburgh. In *Allegheny County v. American Civil*

Liberties Union (1989) (Blackmun), the Court declared unconstitutional the display of a crèche all by itself on the main-staircase of the county courthouse. A majority followed Justice O'Connor's approach, noting that Pittsburgh's display of the crèche without other, non-religious, symbols nearby had the effect of endorsing Christianity. A somewhat different majority then upheld an outdoor display that included a menorah because it was mixed in with seasonal rather than religious symbols. The Court stated: "Whether the key word is 'endorsement,' 'favoritism,' or 'promotion,' the essential principle remains the same. The Establishment Clause, at the very least, prohibits government from appearing to take a position on questions of religious belief or from 'making adherence to a religion relevant in any way to a person's standing in the political community.' " **What's the Takeaway? It is possible to discern what is sometimes called the "Reindeer Rule"—public displays celebrating Christmas are constitutional as long as they include a sufficient amount of non-religious symbolism.** The various opinions reveal little consensus on the Court, however. The membership of the Court has changed almost entirely since *Allegheny County*, but the appearance of two blocs on the Court talking past each other in this area is unchanged.

One highly controversial Establishment Clause challenge to an almost universal daily expression of religion was ended without a decision on the merits in *Elk Grove United School District v. Newdow* (2004) (Stevens). An atheist challenged the daily recitation of the Pledge of Allegiance in his daughter's public school because of the phrase "one nation, under God." A lower court ruled that the phrase constituted unconstitutional establishment, essentially a very short version of the prayers found unconstitutional in the school prayer cases of the 1960s. This threw gasoline on the culture wars, as political conservatives saw opposition to the pledge to be anti-American, at least during wartime. Perhaps wisely, the Supreme Court ended the controversy by concluding that Newdow lacked standing to challenge the pledge. Since then, even some justices who have been quite cautious about allowing public use of religious symbols have defended the pledge, which appears safe from a successful constitutional challenge.

Other cases from the same period reveal a similar set of divergent beliefs about the Establishment Clause and religious symbolism. In *McCreary County v. American Civil Liberties Union* (2005) (Souter), the Court struck down displays of the Ten Commandments on the walls of county courthouses. A majority applied *Lemon,* concluding that the purpose of the display was clearly religious, at least on the record in the case (which included fairly transparent actions to surround the Ten Commandments with historical documents under the impression that would immunize the display under the Christmas precedents). The majority emphasized the connection to the endorsement principle, noting that "showing a purpose to favor religion . . . sends the message to non-adherents 'that they are outsiders, not full members of the political community, and an accompanying message to adherents that they are insiders, favored members.'"

On the same day, however, in *Van Orden v. Perry* (2005), the Court upheld a display of the Ten Commandments on the grounds of the Texas State Capitol. There was no majority opinion, and the plurality opinion expressed the views of those justices who had dissented in *McCreary County.* The "decider" as a practical matter was Justice Breyer, who seemed to swing back to the rationale of the Christmas display cases by emphasizing that the monument was one of many on the capitol grounds and that there was no history of interpreting the mere presence of the Ten Commandments as endorsing a religious message. **What's the Takeaway? One can do a careful lawyer's job and identify narrow distinctions between these displays that arguably justify the opposite rulings. Or one can acknowledge that the contemporary Supreme Court has** found no consensus approach to deciding such cases, resulting in legal theory by "whatever works" for five or more justices. And in *Van Orden,* as in so many other areas of Constitutional Law, no single legal approach is truly a majority conclusion.

Why do we read and discuss these cases? It would be nice to identify a coherent line through these and other cases that reveal the meaning of the Establishment Clause, one that would allow law students to discern the prevailing argument in most cases, and that would enable attorneys to predict the outcome of establishment cases with confidence. But that ain't gonna happen! Sorry.

THINGS TO KNOW
<ul><li>Governments may not favor one religion over another or religion over non-religion.</li><li>The three-part *Lemon* test: secular purpose, primary or principal effect neither helping nor hindering religion, no excessive entanglement. **Then** remember that it only applies when courts decide to apply it.</li><li>Prayers in public schools sponsored or organized by the schools or government are probably Establishment Clause violations. (Wholly voluntary prayer by individual students on their own initiative, on the other hand, would seem to constitute free exercise).</li><li>Public spending for secular educational purposes is usually constitutional, even if the funds end up going to religious institutions.</li><li>Governments may use religious speakers and prayer at public events intended for adults but not at schools or functions intended for children.</li></ul>

- Government may use religious symbols, at least where they are used in a context that avoids the appearance of government endorsement of religion.

- One person's free exercise is another person's establishment. Live with it.

THINGS TO THINK ABOUT

- Is it possible to identify a consistent threat about when to apply the Establishment Clause to official actions that support religious activities?

- Is the problem in finding coherent rules the fact that there are just too many possible settings for Establishment Clause issues to rise, or that the Court has been unwilling to follow prior decisions? (Or both?)

Final Words

We hope you've enjoyed this overview of the First Amendment.

We don't present some grand unified theory that answers all questions, because . . . there isn't one. Instead, there are a variety of reasons for the several rights found in the First Amendment, and you don't have to do mental gymnastics in order to see how they apply in most cases. Probably the shortest statement of what the First Amendment is all about is this: *The Constitution protects the power of individual people to think, to believe, to speak, to criticize, and to have religious faith, or not.*

Students sometimes fear the First Amendment because even more than most other areas of Constitutional Law, it is hard to get a firm footing. Pick your metaphor: mud, thin ice, quicksand, or perhaps all of the above. Let that be a strength. As there are many ways to analyze a problem, no one really expects every student or attorney or even judge to get it exactly right. Often students who turn out to get higher exam grades than they expected will say something like, "How could I get an A? I saw some issues I couldn't fully understand, let alone perfectly answer." The answer to that question is that the exam deserved an A *because* the student recognized that there were things she couldn't fully answer.

We're biased, but we believe the First Amendment may be the most interesting subject in the law school curriculum. Even if you find the legal problems difficult, or if you're not a Con Law junkie like us, you can't beat the stories or the scenery. The cases are just one long collection of heroes and rogues bent on testing the policies discussed in chapter 1—the marketplace of ideas, self-governance, autonomy and the like. The experiences of those persons in the Supreme Court draw the lines between government power and personal liberty as well as you can find anywhere. They also illustrate changes over time. Anti-war speeches that sometimes resulted in long prison sentences a hundred years ago now pass largely unnoticed. The First Amendment is interpreted more expansively today than at any time in our history, and that is probably true for each component part, from the religion clauses to the petition clause.

Some people, however, question the practical importance of studying the First Amendment. One of Bob's colleagues says "Real lawyers do Secured Transactions, not the First Amendment." While many lawyers *do* secured transactions, we are glad to focus here. The worst day in First Amendment law presents more interesting questions than the best day in some boring code specialties. Yes, that's our opinion, but we bet you will (or already do) agree!

Fortunately, lots of lawyers *do* get up in the morning and head to work with energy and a real sense of purpose to handle First Amendment issues. There are some obvious jobs like that: in-house attorneys for media companies and artistic organizations, staff attorneys at the American Civil Liberties Union, legal counsel for organized religions, etc. All these lawyers have a steady diet of the First Amendment in their work. But that is just the start. Thousands of lawyers who work in public law offices consider First Amendment issues all of the time. Legislatures at all levels pass numerous laws that restrict speech, and lawyers draft and defend those laws. Anyone who works as a town solicitor knows how often speech or religion problems arise in representing municipal governments. School districts, police departments, and zoning boards keep them hopping with matters such as speech or dress codes, choice of commencement speakers, parade permits, and special use permits. Many, perhaps most, federal and state attorneys come across First Amendment issues in a wide variety of cases. And each of these settings brings private attorneys into First Amendment controversies to represent government employees disciplined for their speech, students, land-owners, protestors, and businesses facing consumer notification requirements.

Here are two short stories from the early 2000s that illustrate how the First Amendment interjects itself into national debates. One involves Cindy Sheehan, whose son was killed in action while serving in the U.S. Army in Iraq. She became convinced that the war had been a mistake and protested at the White House, Pres. Bush's home in Texas, the U.S. Capitol, the United Nations, and at numerous events. Arrested on several occasions and prosecuted to verdict on some of them, she became an advocate for ending the Middle East wars and for bringing the troops home. Around the same time, the Westboro Baptist Church began conducting protests at funeral services of American soldiers killed in those wars. Their very different message was that God was killing American soldiers in vengeance for the nation's tolerance of homosexuality. Both Ms. Sheehan and the Westboro group defended their protests on First Amendment grounds. Ms. Sheehan was a widely sympathetic figure who avoided conviction, largely because her protests were protected political expression. Despite the contempt the justices openly felt for the exceptionally offensive action, the Supreme Court ruled in favor of the Westboro protests on similar First Amendment grounds.

But the outcomes in specific cases are not the point. In both situations, the several prosecutions of Ms. Sheehan and the various efforts to stop the funeral protests, most of the attorneys on each side were generalist attorneys from small firms or public law offices. Those attorneys had to master very complicated legal principles in a short time and make arguments in a nation that was sorely tempted to follow emotion rather than law. Did the right side win each case? That's not for us to judge. But the cases were decided by law, not politics, and judges respected the principles of free expression, and that's good enough for this imperfect world.

And maybe that's the key to the First Amendment. While (or because) it's not static, it is impossible to master. But it's endlessly fascinating to try. Moreover, lawyers get to take a leading role in helping the world become better bit by bit, and case by case. We're glad you have joined us in this adventure.